Upland
Kirkley

D0295749

HORSE&HOUND
HORSES
of a
LIFETIME

HORSE&HOUND

HORSES
of a
LIFETIME

ADELLA LITHMAN

J. A. Allen
London

British Library Cataloguing-in-Publication Data.
A catalogue record for this book is available from the British Library.

ISBN 0.85131.728.6

Published in Great Britain in 1998 by
J. A. Allen & Company Limited,
1 Lower Grosvenor Place, Buckingham Palace Road,
London, SW1W 0EL.

Typeset and designed by Judy Linard
Printed by Dah Hua Printing Press Co. Ltd., Hong Kong

Horse & Hound is published every Thursday by the Country & Leisure Group, IPC
Magazines Ltd, King's Reach Tower, Stamford Street, London SE1 9LS. For
subscription enquiries and overseas orders call 01444-445555 (fax no 01444-445599).
Please send orders, address changes and all correspondence to: IPC Magazines Ltd,
Oakfield House, 35 Perrymount Road, Haywards Heath, West Sussex RH16 3DH. All
cheques should be made payable to IPC Magazines Ltd. Alternatively, you can call the
subscription credit card hotline (UK orders only) on 01622 778778.

Picture acknowledgments

Most of the photographs in this book are the copyright property of IPC Magazines.
In the other cases permission has been granted by the owners to reproduce them in the book.
There are some photographs for which due to the age of the material, and despite our best
efforts, we have been unable to trace ownership. If anyone has claim to any of the copyright
and can prove ownership, please contact the publishers.

Foreword

Those of you who have read Adella Lithman's 'Horse of a Lifetime' column in *Horse & Hound* will know that these special horses come in many guises. They are not all hugely successful competition horses, Olympic medal winners or Grand National heroes. They may be humble hunters who never missed their turn, one of those incredible ponies that can jump fences they cannot even see over, or just a special character.

The common and golden thread that joins them is their relationship with their rider. With all these horses who have indelibly imprinted their personalities on their human partners, there has been a natural empathy which has allowed horse and rider to communicate almost telepathically. I doubt if we are all lucky enough to have had a horse of a lifetime, but most of us will have enjoyed magical moments when we have managed to instantly communicate with a horse riding with the light contact that is often referred to as a silken thread. I have been lucky enough to have ridden many hirelings over the years and just occasionally have found one which was made for me.

I have lost count of the number of times a hunter hireling has saved my neck by finding that fifth leg, or seen that treacherous strand of barbed wire that I had missed. One spring in the mountains of Wyoming I was caught in the middle of a snowstorm and had to trot for 16 miles in ever-deepening snow to get to the safety of a ranch house. We were literally frozen stiff when we finally arrived.

Never have I been so grateful to a horse. Horse riding is and always will be a risk sport and it is the sharing of the risks that sometimes forges the partnerships that Adella writes about so eloquently. In some circumstances horses do literally save your life.

Adella Lithman's writing in the 'Horse of a Lifetime' column demonstrates the lightness of touch with which we all wish we could ride. As a horsewoman of considerable experience, she has a natural empathy with both the humans and the horses who are the subject of her articles and this shines clearly through. If you ride long enough you will have that bad fall, as Adella can testify, and this explains her natural sympathy. I can recall visiting Adella in hospital, when she had broken both legs in a horrific accident, and all she could think about was that her horse needed work and she was missing out on going to such and such a show. Having recovered after many painful months, she immediately set about getting fit to ride the same horse. Despite the accident, the bond had not been broken.

Readers of *Horse & Hound* are first and foremost horse lovers, so it is not surprising that Adella's column is one of the most avidly read pieces in the magazine. I hope you will enjoy reading this collection of articles about some truly remarkable horses as much as I did.

Arnold Garvey,
Editor, *Horse & Hound*.

Why Geoff is still in rhapsodies over "Rodeo"

Known for his penchant for lazing in bed, Geoff Billington
would have to get up very early to get the better of Rhapsody,
the horse he refers to as "the old devil"

ON the international show jumping circuit,
Geoff Billington is known as "PM", which
does not dictate a ministerial position, but merely
the time he rolls out of bed.

While other riders are up at the crack of sparrow, diligently doing flatwork and warming up
over fences, Geoff is snuggled down under a
duvet. It is safest there.

For if he tried to school his horse Rhapsody, one
of Britain's top 20 show jumpers, winner of nearly £150,000 and his partner in four of his 20
Nations Cups, the horse would try to kill him —
and the word "kill" is used neither lightly nor for
artistic affect.

The horse is known as "Rodeo" and he and his
rider have come to an understanding.

"He likes his own way," says Geoff, "and I like
to be lazy. In the ring, I am the boss. Anywhere
else, I have 45 per cent control and let him think
he is king, otherwise he makes my life miserable."

The odd couple's successful system on the circuit works thus: Rhapsody permits Geoff's groom
Sue Cowley to take him for a quiet hack in the
morning while Geoff is sleeping.

Then, eight competitors before Geoff is due to
jump — it must be eight, not nine or seven —
Rhapsody sometimes allows Geoff to mount.

"Usually, though, he walks on his hind legs
'clapping', at which point I put my arms around

his neck and bale out. If I stayed there and fought
him, he would only stay up longer. I take his reins
over his head and lunge him for two minutes
(you could actually clock this on an egg-timer)
and try and mount again."

There is time remaining for only one practice
jump before entering the fray. In Vienna, though,
for a CSIO, "PM" felt guilty about sleeping in and
thought he would school his horse properly in the
morning. He only mildly asked Rhapsody to
change legs, and the spine-chilling result of the
horse's "broncing" fury brought photographers
running.

In Berlin for a World Cup qualifier, Geoff was still
trying to get Rhapsody to let him mount as the
steward was summoning them forward to jump.

The quiet-life rules regarding Rhapsody are simple. He can never be worked at home. He can
only hack safely alone and he will not travel in
the rear of a lorry, no matter how tight the space.
Any deviation from these regulations results, says
Geoff, "in the horse trying to commit suicide and
taking the nearest person with him".

Rhapsody, who has jumped in most arenas
between Hungary and the Horse of the Year
Show, loathes Hickstead.

"I think," remarks Geoff, "he runs at the fences
with his eyes closed!"

The 16.2hh bay gelding of unknown breeding

was bought in Ireland by the Belgian dealer Francois Mathy and brought a new meaning to the word megabucks — as Sally Mapleson, the former leading lady show jumper, was to discover when she tried him.

He bucked her off and Sally, now married to Mark Heffer, says, mystified: "I do not know how Francois sweet-talked me into having him. It must have been that continental accent."

At their first unaffiliated show, Sally failed to encourage Rhapsody over the first fence. Steve Hadley, who was helping her at the time, took over.

When he finished, he declared sternly: "I strongly advise you to sell this horse, and do not ever ask me to ride it again."

Sally, however, persevered and took the horse to Grade A, hung up her boots and gave Nick Skelton the choice of one of two horses, Airborn or Rhapsody. He tried both for a while and chose Airborn. Rhapsody was offered to Geoff Billington, who, on hearing of the gift horse, decided to consult with his chum John Whitaker.

'John is good at getting inside a horse's head and understanding the way it wants to go. He said the more the horse is restricted, the more it will fight. 'You cannot work him methodically or correctly'."

Heeding the sage's words, Geoff dispensed with draw-reins and balancing reins, threw away the text books and went to war for three

months with no ammunition whatsoever.

"You cannot chastise Rhapsody," he says, "because it makes him more angry. He can buck like anything, rear and spin."

Lancashire-born Geoff, based now at Knutsford in Cheshire, is one of the warmest hearted among Britain's top show jumpers. The son of a foam rubber factory manager began riding at the local stables when he was nine and received his first break by taking over Graham Fletcher's former ride Talk Of The North.

He is 40 now, married to blonde Julie with three small sons. Geoff is a comedian, known for his horseback cabaret in which he mimics the styles of other riders. Even with his sense of humour, he found it difficult to see the funny side of Rhapsody. He eventually waved the white flag at the horse and settled down to an uneasy truce.

Their achievements since 1988 fill three foolscap sheets of around-the-globe successes in Grand Prix, World Cup and Derby classes. Sally Mapleson gives the jockey all credit.

"The horse is quirky and will not be dominated. Geoff has this knack of being able to get on any horse and adapt to it, rather than expecting the horse to adapt to him."

Geoff and Rhapsody will be making music in Germany, Holland, the Royal Lancashire Show and then the Millstreet Derby this summer.

Times, however, are moving on and Rhapsody, at 17, is not getting younger. Geoff has a powerful new rising star, It's Otto, who was his partner in the recent winning Nations Cup team at Hickstead, and of whom he wryly comments: "I have to get out of bed early for him."

It looks as if Otto and Geoff will be at the European Championships, while Rhapsody will be taking it easy by competing only in this country in future. When Rhapsody retires, he will remain with Geoff.

"He has been fantastic for me," says Geoff. "I have had him the longest and he is certainly the toughest. I have always relied on him when I have been short of horses and we must have been around the world seven times, which should make him the British horse with most miles on the clock.

"Rhapsody is an old devil," he says, "but I love him."

29 June 1995

The horse who would try to jump a house

Hunter trials specialist Blackjack often scared his rider witless — but he also saved her life

BLACKJACK, never a horse to hang about, violently leapt off the bridlepath as the sheep in the bushes suddenly picked up their long woolly skirts and fled rippling across the field.

It was normal skittish behaviour from the Thoroughbred and his rider Sharon Dick usually sat with regal composure, only, this time, his leap sent them plummeting into an icy 40ft-deep reservoir.

Sharon, in hard hat, thick sweaters, quilted jacket and new Hunter boots, was not dressed for swimming. Horse and rider surfaced, gasping for breath, with Sharon still hanging on to the reins. She was being dragged down by the weight of her saturated clothing and, to add to her terror, Blackjack was steering a course towards the middle, instead of making for the side.

Clinging to his neck and keeping the reins in a vice-like grip, Sharon struggled to turn him towards a sloping bank and today is able to remark casually: "He is not the greatest of swimmers. We kept going under and coming back up again, but I would not be here if it was not for Blackjack."

On that snowy winter morning in April 1995, Sharon was fighting for her life.

The horse eventually came to rest at the bottom of a steep slope and she led him along this precarious route, with water lapping at their feet, until they reached a gradual incline, which took them gently back to the path. With her new boots gone the way of the *Titanic*, she rode the two miles home dripping wet and in her socks.

Neither of them caught so much as a sniffle, but the incident left Sharon nervous of swimming, while Blackjack, the lightning raider of the northern hunter trials scene, did not turn so much as one of his jet-black hairs the next time he faced water in competition.

The horse went on to win a special PDSA award for helping save his owner and I now wonder if it is right to point out that he was responsible for trying to drown her in the first place. That aside, he received an Heroic Pet Patient Award, which in his special case should have been cited as the Heroic Pet Impatient Award.

Blackjack stoked his own engine in competition and would not wait for Sharon to collect her stirrup irons before bucking mightily and heading for the first fence.

He was a Captain Morgan, sailing with a full wind behind him, plundering silver treasure for Sharon to place on the sideboard. There were as many as 30 rose bowls and trophies a season, some reappearing there for the fourth time in a year.

Sharon recalls a rider, with a smile, threatening to let down the tyres of her lorry to sabotage Blackjack's next sortie, while Sharon's mother Mary once saw a fan — who followed them from course to course — fall from a post and rail fence because he took both hands off the top rail to punch the air in delight as Blackjack skipped through a trappy combination.

Between Blackjack's 12th and 19th birthdays, he won 168 hunter trials at a non-stop pace and in times which often had officials checking their figures in disbelief.

stated that he was 16hh, 10 years old and warned he was not a novice ride.

It took his owner two minutes to realise the extent of his buck and spin and another two years to establish brakes, steering and the fact that he was intolerant of dressage and coloured poles.

At their first hunter trials, Blackjack unloaded her. At their second attempt, he made a unilateral decision to take a short cut through trees, where his rider was swept away by branches.

Undeterred by these hiccoughs, Sharon immediately entered him in the open, agreed with him that the wood had been a good idea for a short cut, remembered to duck and won, fine-tuning the extensive programme for the future, which was highlighted by qualifying four times for the British Airways finals in 1986.

"He would jump a house for me," said his doting owner, who had to mop up the bits after he tried to jump a police car. It happened after vandals broke the gate into Blackjack's field and he and six others bolted.

A police car straddled a main road in a bid to stop them, sending three one side, three the other and Blackjack over the top, with his hooves smashing a window, narrowly missing a sergeant.

The vet who sewed Blackjack together with 200 stitches, doubted he would live, but had not reckoned on the tenacity of Sharon's nursing skills which she offered morning and evening, every day for three months.

Sharon now show jumps under rules and Blackjack contentedly grazes with another pensioner pal called The Flockton Grey, who was the subject of a Jockey Club and police inquiry after a racing scandal about a ringer.

Sharon has all the cuttings but that, as they say, is another story.

'Sometimes," says Sharon, "I would come into some of the fences thinking 'Oh my God,' and Blackjack would be thinking 'Yes please, let's go for it'."

Sharon Dick epitomises the spirit which makes Britain great when it comes to horses.

She was a pony-mad child taken for Saturday lessons to the nearest riding school, which was 20 miles away, and she tormented a neighbouring child who owned a pony. Sharon followed the girl everywhere on a bicycle and was sometimes permitted to ride the pony downhill, after she had first wearily biked to the top.

At 12, she was given her own pony and, today, the petite, dark-haired 30-year-old is a rep for a greetings card company and lives with her parents in a bungalow opposite their stables and land near Sheffield. She has circumvented the irksome problem of shoeing bills by announcing her engagement to James Alton, a farrier.

Blackjack, by No Mercy out of Rose Blanche, is 22 and retired, an ex-hurdler who was pin-fired, turfed out of racing and lucky not to be tinned.

Sharon was 18 when she bought Blackjack through an advertisement in a local paper which

Punctual Pandur who refuses to retire

John Parker reflects on the forceful personality of his nearside
leader of his carriage driving team of four

PARKER and Pandur have a biblical relationship on the lines of Ruth and Naomi.

"Whither thou goest," Ruth said to her mother-
in-law, "I will go." Except, with Parker and
Pandur, there can be a tussle over directions.

Take, for example, the annual carriage driving
job of conveying law lords to the opening session
of the Norwich courts. The route has always followed through the arch of the city's cathedral and
turned left into Old Red Lion Street.

John Parker, the accomplished whip, and
Pandur, his nearside leader, had sailed through
this sea of concrete without a storm for donkeys'
years — until new courts were built. This meant a
new right turn into Palace Street.

With a full load of judges on board, the team
came trotting majestically under the arch, with
Pandur resolutely pulling left to the old courts
and Parker, with gritted teeth, uselessly steering
right.

As far as the horse was concerned, he had seen
the judges climb aboard — he always swivels his
head round to check out passengers — and men
wearing wigs clearly indicated left.

Since neither man nor beast would give in, they
came to an embarrassing halt. Pandur set his feet
and refused to budge until a liveried groom
jumped down and hauled the grumpy horse
around the corner.

"I felt a complete twit," says John. "That horse
knows too much. He knows all the routes. Even if
they are the wrong ones."

There are other minimal disagreements between
Parker and Pandur.

Parker, being a full-blooded male, likes nothing
better than to see a troupe of mini-skirted drum
majorettes twirling their batons. The sight gives
Pandur an apoplectic fit. So do Scots pipers in
kilts.

"He does not mind them in tartan trews," says
Parker, "but not the skirts.

"Last time he saw some, he worked himself into
such a state that he got laminitis all round and I
had to take him to the Newmarket vet. They said
he had got so much adrenalin going he had
brought it on himself."

Pandur is also intolerant of bad time-keeping.
He was taking part in an international ceremony
at Portsmouth once and had two dress rehearsals,
which both lasted precisely 17 minutes.

On the day, Maori dancers overran their allotted
time. Pandur would not tarry and, at 17 minutes
to the second, he was off, necessitating quick
action from a groom, who got a kick in the stomach for her trouble.

Man and horse came together for some of the
best years of their lives.

John Parker was going to follow his grandfather's dream of being a jockey, until his father
dragged him away from Newmarket and settled
him down in a proper job as a sheet-metal worker. After his apprenticeship, Parker joined the
Army, where he learned the art of four-in-hand
driving.

When he hung up his uniform, he established
the Swingletree equestrian establishment, near
Diss, Norfolk, funding it with his earnings as a
carriage driver on films.

The £750 he had saved for centrally heading his home in the freezing winter of 1973 was used to buy Pandur instead of radiators.

This grey sports horse, by a Thoroughbred stallion, hails from Lajosmirzse (pronounced Liarschmitzer) in Hungary. Standing 16.3hh with PT branded on his neck, Pandur was to flourish under John's reign as a star.

It was to be easy to identify Pandur out of four matching greys because three of them, including the driver, would be looking where they were going, while Pandur would be looking into the nearest camera lens.

"He likes attention so much," says John, "that I was giving some people a lesson around the village when Pandur spotted a queue for the jumble sale. 'That's my crowd', said the horse and went and parked himself by it. 'Lord Muck' had arrived."

Together, they have performed the serious and the bizarre, from on stage in *Carmen* to representing Britain a dozen times in the world and European driving trials championships. Until 1982, they would either be competing under FEI rules or taking part in something like the opening of a new shopping precinct.

Then, when Norwich Union sponsored John Parker's historic Royal Mail coach, much charity work was added to their list. Pandur even won a show jumping competition and in one of the man and horse's madder moments, hunted a carriage on stubble behind the local Harriers, until Pandur had to be fought off from taking on one of the ditches.

They hold two Guinness world records, with Pandur taking part in both the 17hr 14min dash from Bristol to London, and a televised 21.63secs change of teams.

Last year, John Parker officially retired Pandur at Olympia, the Christmas extravaganza in which the horse has participated every year since 1976. It seemed like a good idea at the time.

John, 55, put the horse out to grass and Pandur was back in the stable before John returned to the yard. He had kicked his way through the gate.

John tried again, only this time the horse beat him to it by opening the gate.

"Silly old fool," says John. "He still has not twigged that he is 26. He thinks he's four. His whole life has been exciting, with different people

From the box seat, Pandur is the left leader

and places, and he does not want to give it up."

Now, when John has to take horses and carriages away in the lorry, he sends Pandur riding or driving in the village with one of the Swingletree grooms so that he does not feel left behind.

"I tried leaving him in his stable and he had such a tantrum because he was not going with us that I thought he would give himself a heart attack."

"Pandur," says his doting owner, "is an extrovert. You can only have one like him in a team. He is the bravest horse I have ever known across country.

"He was so clever he would think out the hazards for himself. He has been a third of my life and I not only love him, but respect him. The day he dies, I will take a bottle of whisky and drink myself into oblivion."

27 July 1995

Why I'm head over heels for "Dear Boris"

Mary King fondly recalls the horse with the propelling tail
who helped to make her name. He retires this week

THE letter had a North of England postmark and was succinctly and unhelpfully addressed to "King Boris, Devon".

Clearly, though, Her Majesty's Post Office knew of the horse with the regal name, for the letter asking for a souvenir of King Boris's tail was promptly delivered to Mary Thomson's yard at Salcombe Regis, near Sidmouth.

Mary has received hundreds of similar requests down the years, and, had she complied with them all, King Boris, or "Dear Boris", as she refers to him, would now be wishing he had been left with at least one strand with which to flick away the flies.

King Boris was the equine equivalent of Take That, East 17 or any other pop group small girls go gaga over.

He completed 83 horse trials in his career, was placed in 76 of them, finished in the top four in 54 and was one of the few to have chalked up more than 1,000 BHS points.

These statistics, however, did not impress his starry-eyed little fans, who sent him peppermints through the post, and, in return, wanted locks of his hair and signed — or rather hoof-printed — photographs.

They loved him for his tail, continuously circling in competition like an electric fan, distinguishing him from thousands of other event horses.

Three weeks ago, Mary Thomson, who called the horse King after her boyfriend David King, and Boris after a favourite old lorry, loaded up the horse and drove him to her friend Bimmy Amor, who will hunt him with the Taunton Vale. At 16,

King Boris was officially retired from eventing.

Much has happened since Mary acquired the £3,500 7/8 Thoroughbred as a five-year-old, after spotting an advertisement in *Horse & Hound*.

She had been a working pupil with Sheila Wilcox, and then established her own yard in run-down cowsheds, striving as a part-time gardener, butcher's delivery driver and home help to subsidise the new horse business.

She and her mother Jill, treasurer of the Axe Vale branch of the Pony Club, even hand-built the outdoor school — back-breaking, but not heart-breaking, like having to sell good horses she had brought on in order to survive.

Mary could have hated Boris for his tail though, as it cost them full honours at the 1989 Badminton. They were clear across country and in the show jumping and, in the eyes of two judges, were the leaders in the dressage. The third judge was not impressed and marked Boris down for his energetic tail.

When they finished second, pipped by Ginny Leng, the dressage judge apologised and gave them top marks the following year.

It was too late. King Boris was a British Open Champion, a prolific winner of one-day events, but always the page-boy and never the bridegroom at three-day events.

King Boris, the former show hunter bred by Lady Anne Younger — whose son owns Desert Orchid — was the first decent horse Mary Thomson could afford to keep.

Now she is 34, Mrs King, Olympic rider, European and world team gold medallist, winner of five three-day events in a row, including Badminton, with King William, has three horses on the list for the European Championships in Italy.

Mary says that King Boris, the horse she has kept longer than any other, was one of the contributing factors to her success.

"I have had horses who were twice as talented," she exclaims, "but have not done as well because their hearts were not in the right place, like Boris's.

"I learned so much with him. When I made major mistakes, he was always totally forgiving and still tried his hardest to get me out of them.

"One of the worst falls I had was at Badminton's Normandy Bank in 1988, because I came in on a holding stride, making it impossible to jump the fence properly. He went head over heels and I was knocked out for 20 minutes. The next event was at Frome and he won. He has been that sort of horse all the way through."

The 16.3hh bay gelding, co-owned by Gill Robinson and sponsored by Frizzell, is by the HIS stallion Rapid Pass out of Miss Mandy, a 3/4-bred hunter mare of whom it was said that no day was too long, nor any jump too high.

When the fair-haired 5ft 7ins event rider saw him, she thought he was utterly gorgeous and fell for his big eyes, big ears and big attitude.

"He wanted to be busy at something, but did not quite know what," she recalls.

While she thanks Boris for helping her attain her artistry, Lady Anne Younger gives all the praise to the rider.

"People spend time and money breeding good horses," she comments, "but it always comes down to the luck of the draw who gets them. This talented horse could have gone to someone else and done nothing. It is entirely due to Mary Thomson that he has been such a success."

There is a tidy fortune in silverware on sideboards because of this partnership, trophies for the rider with the most points, a couple for the horse with the most points and one for the best English-bred eventer.

There is also Boris's empty stable in Mary's yard.

"He was always first to whinny in the morning, the one most glad to be fussed over by visitors and the horse I trusted most with the students. It feels terrible without him," Mary says feelingly.

10 August 1995

The demon who turned into a dressage dream

Christopher Bartle recalls his triumph in reschooling the renegade
Wily Tout to become one of Britain's best ever dressage horses

THE advertisement had clearly been economical with the truth. "Bold across country"
actually meant an unstoppable, white-knuckle
ride, avoiding all jumps.

The horse had apparently been eventing and
point-to-pointing and finally finished lying upside
down in a ditch on the verge of an equine nervous
breakdown, with the vendor underneath him.

Now the object of the for sale sign was being
tried by a young rider from the future British
team, who refused him after discovering the only
way to bring him to a halt had nothing to do with
a horseman's manual and everything to do with
aiming him at the barn wall.

Christopher Bartle knew none of this when he
innocently travelled from Yorkshire to Hampshire
in the autumn of 1974 to take the five-year-old
horse on a six-month loan, with an option to buy
him for £1,400.

At home the next morning, he brought out the
tack and saw the horse immediately begin to
tremble and then sweat. He was as forward going
as a Porsche without brakes in the indoor school
and Christopher ran him into a corner, wondering what his mother Nicole, a translator of
German dressage books and stickler for correct
riding, would say.

After two weeks indoors, finishing each session
with the gelding dripping with sweat,
Christopher clipped him. It was like the dance of

the seven veils, each chunk of mammoth, woolly
hair falling away, revealing the real Wily Trout, a
16.3hh, quality middleweight, $\frac{7}{8}$th bred, with a
beautiful head and kind, intelligent eyes.

Today at 43, this managing director of the
Yorkshire Riding Centre, and dressage trainer to
Britain's three-day-event teams for the European
Championships and Olympics, admits: "I fell in
love with the horse that moment."

Their remarkable relationship was to have a pro-
found effect. It gave Britain its highest dressage
place ever at the Olympics.

Christopher Bartle went to public school, gained
an economics honours degree, rode in point-to-
points and under Rules, evented his mother's riding school horses and spent a year training with a
former chief riding master of Saumur, the French
equivalent of the Spanish Riding School.

At the end of this varied education, the 6ft jockey, now married with two children, wanted most
to specialise in horse trials.

Wily Trout, ferocious-looking but all bluff in the
stable, was to be his partner, provided he could be
persuaded over a ditch. It took the quivering
horse 20 minutes to step across 2ft and after that
he never stopped at any obstacle.

Stopping him was always the problem. Four
months after Christopher purchased him, they
were in Northumberland for a two-day event.

"He did the steeplechase on his own because I

could not stop him," says Christopher, laughing. "We went without a check on to the roads and tracks. On the cross-country I managed to control him until three fences from home which we cleared at an angle, went through the finish, straight through a string, into the car park."

They finished eighth.

At Bramham for the first time, they winged their way around a corner and came upon a coloured horse which had refused at Sam's Crossing. Wily Trout jumped the rear end of the horse plus Sam's Crossing.

On their second visit to this venue, Christopher failed to turn the fifth-geared Trout after the last fence and soared a white palisade into the spectators, safely clearing a woman sitting on her shooting stick, who fell over backwards.

Wily Trout's eventing career ended in 1976 when he injured a tendon. Christopher's trainer, gold medallist Hans von Blixen-Finecke, recommended they concentrate on dressage, seemingly comical advice since Trout's choppy trot appeared so suspect at vet's inspections that sometimes Christopher was asked to run him up a second time. Besides, the horse was always tense and ready to explode.

Christopher extracted from him a good walk, an expressive canter, combined with piaffe and passage. The trot, however, would always remain his weakness.

The ceaseless battle to settle him down could take hours of work the day before a competition and as many as five hours on the day itself, involving lungeing, walking the horse in-hand around the venue and sessions in the saddle.

They were carving a steady path to the top, but the selectors felt that Wily Trout was too unreliable for the team until July 1980, when they could no longer ignore the pair as they put up the best British performance in the Intermediare I at the substitute Olympics at Goodwood.

In 1984 they were in Los Angeles for the real Olympics and, as they entered the arena, there was a shattering wave of sound from the enthusiastic crowd.

"That," says Christopher, "was a 30-second phase in my life I shall remember until my dying day. I felt the horse tense and grow an inch and I thought he would blow it all out of the water."

Wily Trout gave him the ride of a lifetime and they were sixth. They were also national champions twice and second in the 1986 Dressage World Cup, a position not yet bettered by another British rider.

Eight months ago Wily Trout was put down at home. He was 25. A talented man had lavished affection on this difficult, supercharged equine and Wily Trout had amply repaid him.

17 August 1995

The athlete denied his Olympic chance

Jennie Loriston-Clarke describes how she found the "Dutch courage" needed to ride the founding father of British dressage

THE colt stood white-eyed and screaming at the top of the lorry ramp and, when his feet touched the ground, lifted them straight off again in a violent plunge and rear.

"My goodness," said Jennie Loriston-Clarke with impeccable restraint, "he looks wild. I will need Dutch courage to ride this one."

Jennie was one of the founding mothers of modern day dressage and Dutch Courage became a big daddy of them all, sire of seven graded stallions, winner of 127 dressage competitions, including 32 Grands Prix, eight Grands Prix Specials, and 21 Intermediare IIs.

She found him in a Dutch yard, peering, with difficulty, over a tall stable door. She was on her way home from Frankfurt with her number one dressage horse Kadett, and was accompanied by Herr Franz Rochowansky, the former chief instructor of the Spanish Riding School, hunting for a mare or stallion to bring on.

It was snowing and Dutch Courage's owner, suffering from flu, refused to drag himself from under the duvet to show him to this special customer. Disconsolately, Jennie left, scoured other yards unsuccessfully and returned again, drawn by the colt's noble head. This time, she demanded the vendor arise from his death bed.

Jennie saw the brown horse trotted in-hand along the road, decided he was a cross between Merely-A-Monarch and Laurieston, the leading two event horses of the day, and gave Herr Rochowansky the task of negotiating the price down from £1,000 to £750.

Dutch Courage, 16.1hh by the Thoroughbred

Millerol out of Higonia, moved into Jennie and her husband Anthony's old Brockenhurst yard and was stabled next door to a horse called Ben.

They nicknamed Dutch Courage "Bill" and the pair were known as Bill and Ben, the Flowerpot Men.

Unlike his namesake, Bill was no clumsy string puppet, but constructed of pure elastic and bristling with intelligence.

At four, he was doing Novice classes, at five, he was second in a Medium class, at six, he was doing Prix St Georges. At seven, Bill was making a name for himself for all the wrong reasons at Aachen, where wires attached to electric light poles twanged in the wind like rigging on yachts in a marina, sending him out of collected walk, bolting across the arena.

Jennie next took him on the scholarship she was awarded to train at Warendorf in Germany, where Dutch Courage's athleticism marked him out as an Olympian — an Olympian who, through bad luck and international politics, never entered the Olympic arena.

His rider should have been delighted with his commanding talents.

Initially, however, she felt dismay, because it meant Dutch Courage would be eclipsing her favourite, Kadett, who had taken her to the Munich and Montreal Games.

In 1977l, she retired Kadett with dignity at the age of 16 and let Dutch Courage flourish. The following year, her "Flowerpot Man" won the bronze medal at the World Championships at Goodwood.

"He was the most athletic horse I have ever ridden. I have never felt anything like it," says Jennie, now 52 and bound for the European Championships in Luxembourg with Dutch Courage's son Catherston Dazzler.

"Dutch Courage," she declares, "had a wonderful piaffe."

But in the days when Jennie became seriously involved in dressage, there were merely a handful who could piaffe, while others fumblingly followed.

Also, there were only half a dozen Prix St Georges classes and a couple of Grands Prix a year in Britain and, for those who travelled abroad, it meant journeying by train and walking their horses from city railway stations to show venues, which could prove a stressful experience.

The sport's leaders were glamorous grannies like Lorna Johnstone, who celebrated her 70th birthday by coming 12th at the Olympics.

Jennie, a proponent of freestyle to music, was the new generation, a young mother of two daughters who was among those to propel the discipline into Britain's fastest growing equestrian sport.

Dutch Courage was selected for the Moscow Olympics which were then boycotted by Britain, and again chosen for Los Angeles in 1984, but was taken ill with a virus a week earlier.

"When the Olympic vet came down and did flexion tests, Bill was in absolute agony. It took him three months to recover and he never went again in the way he had before. That is why I retired him from competition the next year."

Bill, however, carried on founding a dynasty of eventing, show jumping and dressage horses. He sired seven graded stallions, the highest number in this country, and among his children and grandchildren are Dutch Gold, Catherston Dutch Bid, Catherston Dazzler, The Clog Dancer, who holds the Asian high jump record of 7ft $2\frac{1}{2}$in, Hogarth, the heavyweight show hunter, and Catherston Dancing Breeze, who won the Royal Show's broodmare class with her winning foal at foot.

The whole list of equine achievers descended from Dutch Courage goes on for pages, even more remarkable since he only ever had around 30 mares a season.

Jennie lives now at the new 350-acre Catherston Stud at Whitchurch in Hampshire — where Dutch Courage's stud card was found in the attic of the Georgian farmhouse when the Loriston-Clarkes moved in — and visitors who fancy a tipple and a rest at the indoor school can go to the Dutch Courage Room and have a drink at Bill's Bar.

Three years ago, on Friday the 13th, Dutch Courage was put down at home after colic. An autopsy revealed that part of his intestines was gangrenous. He had been used in displays and ridden until the day of his death.

"I felt ghastly," Jennie said about his passing, but then she is the sort of person who would say that a hurricane is a slight breeze.

31 August 1985

The "great crack" that was Alverton's first race

Although celebrated for many more famous rides, Jonjo O'Neill
says it is tragic Alverton who still claws at his emotions

THE irrepressible Jonjo O'Neill was torn between describing his relationship with the chestnut gelding as fitting like a bespoke pair of gloves or as divine as the night of his life with a dream woman.

He disposed with the glove idea, choosing the latter in blush-making terms, and then toned it down declaring: "You know when you click with somebody or something, it is magic. It was the same with this horse.

"The first time I popped him over a fence, I knew he was brilliant. He was kind, honest, lovely to sit on and we trusted each other."

The equine idol was Alverton, who won 11 Flat races, five over hurdles and six steeplechases, unhindered by a pair of bowed tendons the size of a girl's arm, powered by a huge heart, and described by the racing press as "tough, genuine and versatile" to a remarkable degree.

Jonjo, son of a Co Cork grocer with pony pictures plastered around his bedroom, founded his career on the back of a protesting pig which he leapt aboard for a few porky bucks when he was eight.

He next turned to stealing rides on donkeys loose in fields at night, running messages and fattening up runts from pig litters until he had enough to buy a £27 pony.

He had Dolly broken in and hunting with the Duhallow by the time he was 10.

At 15, he was an apprentice jockey and at 19 came to England to ride for Gordon Richards, becoming champion jockey twice and setting a record of 149 wins in the 1977-78 season.

Jonjo O'Neill is, in fact, better known for his commanding rides on Sea Pigeon and the legendary Dawn Run, but now, at 43 and a trainer at Ivy House, Penrith, Cumbria, he says that Alverton — by Midsummer Night II — is still the only equine to claw at his emotions, with little Dolly coming a close second.

In front of him on a table in the farmhouse sitting room was Alverton's shoe mounted on an onyx ashtray, and Jonjo, in T-shirt and jeans, recalled the "great crack" that was their first race.

It was soft going at Teeside and there were only two horses in it, Alverton and Kruganko, ridden by his pal Colin Hawkins. Colin's horse fell and brought down Jonjo, although Colin would say it was the other way round.

The pair of them ate dirt out in the country, only too aware of their ludicrous situation, a two-horse race with two fallers, and they were convulsed with laughter.

The result was that Colin was read the riot act by his trainer, and Jonjo was hauled before the stewards, who wanted to know why he had waited for Colin before setting off again; Alverton won.

"I could not believe it," said Jonjo of the debacle and called himself an "eejit" for it.

pink and green, they started favourites, with the horse jumping like a buck on the first circuit.

Around 50 yards before Becher's Brook for the second time, Alverton changed legs and was now approaching the world famous fence on the wrong lead.

Jonjo sat quietly, thinking like hundreds of times before, that the horse would put himself right.

In the next seconds the horse was dead, the pundits saying it was because he took off with a loose horse too close for safety, catching the top of the fence, falling awkwardly and breaking his neck.

Jonjo says that it is rubbish and firmly believes nine-year-old Alverton died of a heart attack, because he did not pick up at the fence, but ran into it and flipped over the top with the momentum.

"I was choked, crying my eyes out. Desperate it was," he says in his soft Irish lilt.

Later in the weighing room, Jonjo, who chalked up a total of 901 winners, was numb to the battering and bruising and vowing never to pick up a saddle again.

Alverton's trainer Peter Easterby, who had the horse in his care since he was a three-year-old, was equally shocked and upset, but magnificently set about rousing the jockey to ride in the last race.

"He did not bully, he just came in with loads of support for me and said that he was as sick as I was.

Jonjo and Alverton polished their act and gelled more smoothly in around another 15 races, especially in 1979, when they took the coveted Cheltenham Gold Cup in a blizzard, which made the reins fiendishly slippery, the goggles useless and the going heavy and slithery.

Alverton was now deemed a "handicap certainty" with only 10st 13lb for the Grand National and with Jonjo in the Snailwell Stud colours of

"Peter said it was a tough old game and you had to keep going."

Today, there are 43 horses in Jonjo's Cumbrian yard and this father of three can look back and say: "Alverton was something special.

"He gave me a fantastic feeling with his arm-wrenching enthusiasm and I am convinced he died doing what he loved most — jumping."

7 September 1995

The "freak" who thought nothing was too big to jump

Richard Walker recalls the "mighty atom" who helped him set
a Badminton record that is still unbroken after 26 years

THE "mighty atom" was considered an equine freak, a titch who strutted like a giant.

He devoured cross-country fences, brought his rider and trainer out in a sweat and was the scourge of Field Masters.

Yet Pasha gave the Olympic rider and four-times national champion Richard Walker a real passion, a career and a record which still holds strong after 26 years.

Richard Walker reigned supreme at Badminton in 1969 when he was only 18, the youngest rider ever to win Britain's premier horse trials.

It is a record unlikely to be smashed, and it is all the more delightful because Richard had been saddled with the horse after no one wanted to buy him, even at a knock-down price of £350.

"Don't laugh," warns Richard, before explaining how Pasha was bred. "By an Arab stallion called Rudan out of a Suffolk Punch/Thoroughbred mare, definitely not the sort of breeding for ideal Badminton material.

"But," says Richard, "I have learned that, in any breed, there are going to be freaks who will achieve superstar status in competitions for which they were not ideally suited.

"Badminton in 1969 was every bit the challenge it is today and, if Pasha were around to do Badminton 1996, he would be as adept as the best of the horses — only more difficult to control."

Pasha, a chestnut gelding with four white socks, stood only 15.1hh and was an equine thug. Had he been human, Pasha would have had pink punk hair, chewed gum with his mouth open and people would have crossed the street to avoid him.

Pasha and Richard came together for a brief period, the right time in their careers, and moulded into a perfect partnership.

South-African born Richard was given riding lessons once a week in Johannesburg and when his British parents returned with him to England, he was encouraged to compete by family friends Claude and Anne Philimore.

The Philimores acquired Pasha from Mark Phillips's aunt Flavia and to the young lad the mighty atom was an opportunity to go from 14.2hh on to a horse, albeit a small one.

In 1965, Colonel Babe Moseley, one of the architects of modern horse trials, spotted the duo at Pony Club and thought them ideal talents for the inaugural Junior European Horse Trials championships. Only two countries participated, but the following year, when 10 teams entered, Richard on Pasha became the silver medallist.

By now, Richard was a working pupil at Lars Sederholm's Waterstock House Training Centre and his parents had purchased Pasha in lieu of their son's school fees, on terms which meant he had to sell the horse after two years.

In 1969, at Haras-du-Pin in France, after finish-

ing second after a gruelling cross-country, the teenage rider, much in awe of Colonel Moseley, remembers the great man gazing at Pasha in his stable.

The colonel was clearly in some sort of reverie and Richard says: "He didn't say anything, just admired him as a freak little horse."

Richard was convinced that his future lay as a professional horseman but, meanwhile, there was still the matter of selling Pasha. He advertised the horse, failing to attract a customer and, on the basis of not knowing what else to do with him, entered him for Badminton.

Fence five was Huntsman's Close, a drop fence into gloomy woods needing a tight right turn to exit out over another fence into clear daylight.

Pasha, however, had his own agenda, spotting a straight run over rails which was still between flags — quite acceptable, but not part of the designed course. Ignoring his rider's attempt to steer a correct line, Pasha took on the rails, nearly unshipping his jockey and breaking the top of the obstacle. It was 5ft 6ins high.

Pasha was retired at the age of 14 to the hunting field where, after clearing a gate on to a road, plus a motor car, and being certified crazy whenever he saw hounds, he was sent to Waterstock, where he proved a tractable schoolmaster. He died when he was 19.

Today, Richard, now 45, based at Point Farm, Strathern, near Melton Mowbray, is diverting from his full-time equestrian interests. He is cutting back on liveries and training riders, while still maintaining a small private string in order to pursue a marketing and distribution business.

After the partnership with Pasha, he went on to win two team gold medals and two individual silvers. He won at Windsor, Bramham, Burghley twice and completed Badminton nine times.

"Pasha," he says, "was tough, careful and overbrave. He was full of dazzle, loved by everyone and, in his own way, a giant of a horse.

"He was the foundation of my passion for horses and the sport, and he taught me that nothing is too big to jump."

14 September 1995

Why Buck did everything but live up to his name

Everyone, including the Queen, asked after Lord Patrick
Beresford's polo pony before enquiring about his
owner's health

IF you catch sight of the handsome Lord
Patrick Beresford in one of the society magazines, there are always strikingly beautiful
women photographed at his side, and the betting is that most of them would have been happy
for him to have felt half as much for them as he
did for his horse.

Lord Patrick was loving and unswervingly
loyal to his horse. Talk to him today, six years
after Buck's death, and Lord Patrick needs a
moment to be rid of the emotional lump in his
throat.

"Buck," he says, "was such a gentleman that if
he thought of bucking he would send a telegram
first, warning you to sit tight. He was an absolutely lovely fellow, so gentle, good natured and what
was remarkable about him was that he was so
good at so many things."

Take a couple of extracts from the "Buck diaries"
and see how the horse's talents merited the sig-
nature tune "Anything Goes".

Saturday night, he and the dashing lord are winning a midnight steeplechase and the next morning are on the polo field taking the Warwickshire
Cup.

Move on, and Buck is at the Royal Windsor
Horse Show, leaving one ring as the champion
heavyweight polo pony and entering another to
jump in a Foxhunter class.

Catch Buck and Lord Patrick in winter and they
would be up with the Duke of Beaufort's hounds,
at one time proudly giving the then three-day-
event World Champions, Ginny Leng and
Priceless, a lead across country.

In 1985, they came third in the Beaufort traditional race and Lord Patrick recalls approaching
the last fence hearing the crowds roaring: "Come
on Buck".

They took off way before the wings and landed
an equal distance the other side.

"It was like lifting off in a rocket," says Buck's
jockey.

Buck had yet another role to play. Lord Patrick
was *chef d'équipe* to the British three-day event
team between 1985 and 1992 and Buck was his
hack while the team was training, upside Ginny
when she was doing her fast work.

Buck was a diamond fit for a royal crown and in
later years nobody bothered to enquire how Lord
Patrick was.

Even the Queen crossed the room once and Lord
Patrick, honoured to be sought by Her Majesty,
was somewhat taken aback by her first words,
which were: "How is Buck?"

Lord Patrick Tristram de la Poer Beresford, son
of the seventh Marquess of Waterford, hunted in
Ireland as a child, then went to Eton, followed by
Sandhurst and the Royal Horse Guards.

Today, he is 61, divorced, living in a peaceful, cosy Berkshire cottage and is the equestrian tour director of the travel company Abercrombie and Kent. He is about to lead a riding safari into Botswana's big game delta and next summer will escort a party of *Horse & Hound* readers to the Olympic three-day event in Atlanta. In his youth, Lord Patrick race-rode, winning 45 point-to-points and five under Rules, but it was as a distinguished high-goal polo player that he came across a cheeky, intelligent foal by the Thoroughbred stallion Djang out of an Argentine mare.

He waited until Buck was three before buying him and the 15.2hh bay gelding proved fast and brave and very eager to learn. Before long, he was playing in all the major high-goal tournaments, was in the winning teams for the Queen's and Cowdray Park Challenge Cup and represented Britain against New Zealand.

Buck, though, was a natural born jumper and it is as a superlative hunter that Lord Patrick remembers him best. The gelding was a horse that Lord Patrick felt an affinity with, so much so that he could "have a conversation", and he always reckoned Buck would have been a poor poker player because he showed all his emotions in his face.

Buck was 15 when he and Lord Patrick had their last and most awful day together.

About 30 yards from a Beaufort fence, Buck seemed to lose his action, jumped stiffly, went

down in front and Lord Patrick knew instantly that his beloved horse was having a heart attack.

His rider tried to vault clear but Buck came down, pinning Lord Patrick's left leg to the ground.

"I shouted, 'Buck, Buck, get up'."

The horse made an enormous effort, sufficient to pull himself clear, after which he lay still.

Says Lord Patrick: "I loosened his girth and, in a pathetic gesture, took off my coat and tried to spread it over him. I was kneeling below his neck, my hands on his face, exhorting him not to give up.

"Then, suddenly, I knew he was gone. Sometime later, with indescribable sadness, I got to my feet and stood gazing down at the best and dearest friend I had ever had."

"Even in death," says Lord Patrick, "Buck looked hauntingly elegant."

21 September 1995

The winning team of Prince and Lord

Race rider and journalist Lord Oaksey formed an unbreakable
22-year partnership with Tuscan Prince — not the best
racehorse, but the one he loved most

I T began with a red-faced, heart-felt apology following an embarrassing nonsense in a Cheltenham steeplechase back in December 1964. Jockey Lord Oaksey had been in the happy posi-

tion of being on one of only two horses still on their feet after seven fallers in the first race of the day.

Confidently steaming down the hill in the lead with two to jump, he suddenly espied a hurdle

in front of him. A hurdle on the steeplechase course?

There was a stomach-churning moment of doubt and he reined in Pioneer Spirit, yelling to Bill Tellwright, the jockey behind, that they must have taken the wrong track. Bill, without a check, gave him a look of pity mingled with contempt and powered victoriously past him to the winning post.

Lord Oaksey, one of Britain's articulate authorities on racing, was open mouthed and incoherent with disbelief.

He would have preferred quietly dying that day. Instead, he was fined £25 by the stewards, subjected to a few choice phrases from disgruntled punters and then thought it best to drive to trainer Roddy Armytage's yard and apologise profusely.

John Oaksey is immensely likeable. It is no surprise that Mr Armytage forgave the erring amateur jockey and even invited him to ride out — which is how Lord Oaksey came to partner a black beauty called Tuscan Prince.

The equine prince and the Lord had a 22-year long relationship, which only ended last year when the horse was put down at the age of 30.

They had raced, hunted and team chased together and Lord Oaksey also entrusted his daughter Sara to Tuscan Prince when she started point-to-pointing at 17.

The sweet-natured 16.1hh gelding made all his riders feel safe and Lord Oaksey, now 66, will not hear a word against him. Brave as a lion, he says, but admits there were limitations. In fact, "Tuscy" was a bit chicken-hearted sometimes, needing leads across tricky Hunt country.

On the track, he liked daylight and made the front running until he had cleared the last, at which point he considered his day's duty done, and switched off.

A sharp crack made no difference, so Lord Oaksey developed an ungentlemanly growl. He gave me an example of this tonsil accelerator while sitting in his paper-strewn study at Hill Farm, Oaksey, near Malmesbury in Wiltshire. It rattled the eardrums and was of sufficient force to provoke an old broken chair into picking up its legs and running. It rarely failed to thrust Tuscy into overdrive, but frightened silly the other horses around him.

Tuscan Prince, by Black Tarquin out of Leney Princess, was ridden by 19 different jockeys, chalking up wins in 13 chases and two hurdle races.

Lord Oaksey rode him 22 times between 1972 and 1975 and, when the horse was retired, his owner Sir John Thomson gave him to the jockey to use as a hunter, because he knew how much he loved him.

For Lord Oaksey was not only a racing man, but a countryman, horseman and someone who felt undressed without a dog trotting at his heels.

After Eton, the Army and Oxford, he quickly realised that, as he followed his father, the first Baron Oaksey and fourth Baron Trevethin, into law, there would be no time to pursue fully what he liked best.

He became a distinguished newspaper, magazine and TV racing journalist, committed to charity work for the Injured Jockeys Fund and, in the beginning, supported his amateur race-riding with the pen.

He rode 200 winners in 20 years, became a leading amateur on the track and notorious for being run away with at home. He took the Imperial Cup, the Whitbread, the Moet et Chandon Silver Magnum four times, the Hennessy, the Kim Muir twice and Foxhunters at both Cheltenham and Liverpool, and was second in the Grand National.

"Tuscy," he says feelingly, "was nowhere near the best, but he gave me more fun and bigger thrills than any other horse. I admired him and adored him."

With his first wife Tory on her mare Blue Bonito and Tuscy sometimes in their slipstream, there was no territory they would not cross.

They ate up VWH country and as the Tory Party team chasers, everyone knew they were the ones to beat.

Tuscy lived at Lord Oaksey's farm for 15 years, pampered and pepperminted and eventually suffered with arthritis in his back legs.

This much-loved horse only blotted his copybook once when he bolted with a secretary. Always one to spring to the Prince's defence, the Lord says with a fond smile: "He only did it for a joke."

28 September 1995

How Craven A lit up Robeson's life

Peter Robeson has fond memories of the 15.2hh mare who
cleared 7ft 4in

BEFORE the vet cut the Thoroughbred colt, he wanted first to cut the roast beef.

"Has he had any mares yet?" inquired the vet.

"No," said the gangly, teenaged Peter Robeson.

"Right," said the vet. "Stick him out in the field with the mares and we'll geld him after we have eaten."

Lunch with the hospitable Robeson family was not to be sniffed at and proved most satisfactory all round.

The vet had a feast, the colt had a Shire mare and a year later, in 1942, Peter Robeson had the result — a bay filly with big feet, called Craven A after a popular brand of cigarettes.

She was affectionately known as "Old Bag" on bad days and "Old Love" on good days. She had the thrust of a Harrier jump jet, at 15.2hh was able to clear 7ft 4in and provided Peter Robeson with a travel ticket around the world, taking on board any reasonable trophy on offer and two Olympic bronze medals.

Craven A dictated the course of Peter Robeson's life.

"Without her," he says, "I might have been a steeplechase jockey, a full-time farmer or head man of a yard. Something to do with animals.

"She started me off in the high profile life of international show jumping, and once I had tried it, I did not want to let it go."

He was jumping in the Pat Smythe, Harry Llewellyn, and Wilf White era and, at 5ft 11in with a thatch of blond hair, grey eyes and ice cubes in his brain, Peter Robeson was considered the most stylish rider of them all.

Today, at 66, he considers Craven A the boldest horse he ever rode — more courageous than Scorchin and Firecrest, who could jump bigger, and certainly more gutsy than Grebe, who had all the cheek.

At home on the 800-acre Fences Farm in Bucks, with his former show jumper wife Renee, he was amused by how values have changed.

He was the first man to win a £100 purse, greeted like a million pounds today, and the first also to take home a car with the red rosette.

"A Renault 4," he exclaims, with emphasis on the "4".

In his day, he rode in more Nations Cups teams than any other British rider, won the Wembley working hunter championship and only ever had one moment of horror when Craven A took off in the New York arena and cleanly jumped a treble combination the wrong way round.

"Nearly made me lose all my hair," he says. "I did think of baling out ...".

Peter's philosophy, which he has passed on to many pupils, was that riding a horse was like painting, ballet or music. An art form which required flowing movement, not imposed movement or restriction.

"I never wanted to be a dictator to a horse. I wanted give and take, with respect on both sides."

All of these ideals were founded on the back of Craven A while he was an apprentice.

"She was my saving grace while I was learning my trade. When starting in jumping, everybody

needs something extra brave and extra honest.

"She often used to meet a fence with orders from me. If I made a silly decision, she said: 'Sorry mate, I'm going to do it my way.' Through her, I learned to do the job efficiently, and to compromise."

In 1948, when Peter was 19 and the Old Love only six, they were invited to train for the Olympic Games.

"We were sent home and told: 'Well done kids, get some experience'."

They were picked as reserves for the 1952

Helsinki Games, and went on to jump in most of the European capitals, Canada, and the USA. Her rider was to have his Olympic successes without her.

Craven A died when she was retired, aged 18, and Peter Robeson, who is on the BSJA training committee and breeds chasers as a hobby, says: "She gave me a career which made me the luckiest man on earth.

"If you are born again, I would like to return to the same place and do it all over again with her."

5 October 1995

Why winning The Jackpot became the rebel's cause

One of Britain's top rock drummers, Kenney Jones, fell in love with a former failed American racehorse he was warned not to buy

IT was the reeling world of money, sex, drugs and rock 'n' roll. But rock drummer Kenney Jones found he could do without the drugs, because he had something else.

The Eastender with gold records says: "Horses and riding kept me sane. They were as good as medication or a psychiatrist. I did not need to do drugs."

He could so easily have been one of the wild men of pop, a rebel who was an under-age driver, a Mod with Parka and a Lambretta too, yet who also held tradition and family ties as values not to squander.

His musical career and love of horses and equestrian sport started in the back room of a Stepney pub.

Kenney was rehearsing with The Small Faces when the keyboard player said he knew of stables where they could hire horses.

To the rest of the band, being towed through woods on lead-reins was another laughter-filled lark. To the teenage drummer, it was the start of an adventure which has taken him hacking, celebrity show jumping at Olympia, hunting with a diamond stud in his ear, to where he is today, a quietly spoken 47-year-old gentleman, a father of five with his own polo club, Hurtwood Park, at home in Ewhurst, Surrey.

Kenney Jones shot to fame with The Small Faces,

continued drumming with the Faces and Rod Stewart and was The Who's choice to replace Keith Moon.

With drumsticks in hand, he was considered a bit of a technician, one of the top five drummers in Britain. With reins in his hand, he proved to be a natural.

All through the touring, adulation and partying, Kenney Jones kept slipping away to stables at home and abroad.

He has hired and owned many horses in the past 30 years, but he hit a winning streak with The Jackpot, a grey Thoroughbred and a former failed American racehorse he was warned not to buy.

Kenney had been playing polo in Palm Beach, Florida, and was looking for a couple of ponies. Jackpot was considered a nutcase.

"I have never believed a horse is no good. It is horses for courses and horses for owners. You have one that is suited to you," he says.

"Jackpot was a problem. He would get into a melee on the polo ground, jump up and down and try to run away.

"I fell in love with the look of the animal and just felt glorious with him. I liked his stride, ideal to hit a ball from, and I though he was freaking out through fear, not because he was a problem horse."

advert run by a charity raising money to save ponies from cruelty."

Jackpot arrived in England in 1990 and was turned out for the winter. He was brought in again looking relaxed and more round.

Kenney recalls: "I played him slowly at the end of the season. I went into the line-up and patted him and stroked him, walked him in and out and played for three minutes instead of seven.

"He is magic now," declares Kenney, "and I love him to death."

Kenney plays off a zero handicap for a variety of teams, including Los Machos (as in lost matches), with two other rock stars, Stewart Copeland from The Police and Mike Rutherford from Genesis.

His charity matches at home have raised thousands of pounds and attracted crowds of 3,500, among them polo playing fans, Jess, 18, and Jay, six, two of his sons.

The elder was a junior member of the Royal Berkshire and played in the Pony Club tournament, while Jay sticks and balls from his pony.

In fact, the only horse Kenney will allow the little boy to ride is Jackpot.

"He has a docile nature and makes everyone feel so safe that I use him to teach people. He can be lazy, but he knows to get down to business when I pick up a good contact.

There was another factor to why the $5,000 Jackpot, standing 15.1hh, came to cross the Atlantic.

Kenney felt sorry for him: "He looked like an

"I can have as much fun hacking. I feel at one with Jackpot, and the feeling is mutual."

12 October 1995

The flying machine who was a true Prince among horses

Pat Smythe's greatest challenge was spirited, athletic and playful, an international sensation who went to the Olympics without her

THE name Pat Smythe means "show jumping". She was simply the best and then there were the rest.

To today's women show jumpers, who compete on level-pegging with the men, Pat was the pathfinder. Her breathtaking performances, which could not be ignored, eventually achieved equal rights for women to represent their country in Nations Cup teams and at the Olympics.

To a nation of pony-loving schoolgirls, Pat Smythe was a heroine. They pasted her pictures on bedroom walls and trotted over cavaletti, pretending to be the great lady rider.

Being a chit of a girl in a man's world was not easy. Her winning was considered an irritant to General Franco when she trounced his Army officers, an impudence by Americans for beating them on a broken-down old racehorse and an embarrassment to the British bigwigs, who chauvinistically decided to take her horse to the 1952 Olympics and leave her behind.

They nearly ruined the gelding, left her in tears, but she fought back, more resilient than ever, full of spirit.

That spirit and pluckiness is still radiating today as Pat Smythe, now 66, battles with heart trouble. She knew she was unwell 10 years ago, but gritted her teeth and said nothing about it as she devotedly nursed her ailing husband to the end.

Only afterwards did she think of her wretched heart, which is still plaguing her today, leaving her weak-voiced and fragile. Ask Pat Smythe, though, about her horse of a lifetime and, as efficient as ever, she has all the information at her fingertips.

In her mind, she is partnering Prince Hal again — in Brussels, clearing a record 7ft 4ins, in Algiers, taking the coveted Gold Buttons after beating the world's all-male Olympic riders, in Lisbon, popping a treble of flimsy 6ft 6ins uprights, in London, winning the Victor Ludorum, and Paris, where a poet wrote: "They disdain the ground."

Pat Smythe was 21, having gone through the junior card and making a name for herself in seniors internationally, when she spotted a 16hh chestnut well down the field ballooning the last fence of the Kim Muir Steeplechase at Cheltenham.

Smitten, she later bought the gelding over the telephone for £150. He was eight, had a "leg", no mouth, could not canter, was highly strung and wrenched her arms out. She could only see athleticism, elegance and playfulness, a loving horse who liked to twang the farrier's braces.

He was the toughest of all her rides and the one who, left to his own devices in front of a fence,

to the team looking round and beautiful, but a couple of months later she was told to pick him up at Badminton, where he stood shivering, thin and miserable.

"They said I could ride him there in the Grand Prix that afternoon, but he was so nervous I couldn't do a thing with him. I put up a 1ft pole and he went crackers."

In tears, she persevered, regained his confidence and then, on the horse the Olympic riders could not handle, went out to beat them all.

Four years later, much to her indignation, Prince Hal was left at home, while, as the first woman Olympic rider, she picked up a team bronze medal with Flanagan.

The world-famous rider, who had also been successfully associated with Tosca, Scorchin, and Finality, quit the saddle in 1963 when she married Sam Koechlin, an Olympic Swiss three-day event rider, doctor of law and the managing director of Ciba-Geigy.

They lived in Switzerland, had two clever daughters and Mrs Patricia Rosemary Koechlin Smythe OBE wrote more than 20 books, occasionally taught children to ride and also acted as *chef d'équipe* to British teams.

would lose his nerve. However, with Pat and her unerring accuracy, Prince Hal knew he could jump the world: "I schooled him, schooled him and schooled him".

The following year, they were a sensation competing internationally and were described in print as the closest combination to a flying machine.

In 1952, Pat Smythe was grounded only because she was a woman, while Prince Hal went to the Olympics without her. He was lent

She is now in England, living in a Gloucestershire farmhouse surrounded by friends and plagued by doctor's appointments for her heart.

Prince Hal, who died when he was 15, still leaps, but only out of dramatic old black and white photographs.

"He was something special," she said. "With me, he knew he could jump the moon."

19 October 1995

Buchan —
the brilliant hunter
with no brakes

Football commentator Jimmy Hill recalls his unforgettable
13-year hunting partnership with the horse who would
jump anything

THE Coventry City manager with one of the most famous jutting jaws, bearded or unbearded, on television, was playing a bizarre game of soccer.

He was on horseback, rolling a giant blown-up quilted ball for charity against National Hunt jockeys. Unsurprisingly, Jimmy Hill, along with his boys, fell off many times, losing the match.

"You don't want to be mucking about like that," said Ted Edgar. "If you really want to ride, come over to my place."

Jimmy Hill duly presented himself at the Warwickshire show-jumping yard the following Tuesday. Ted was absent and his wife, Liz, put him through his first lesson. Later, in the privacy of the loo, Jimmy removed his smart flannel trousers, to find the legs that had won him fame playing football for Brentford and Fulham, looked worse than after a match — they were red-raw on the inside.

"How did your man go?" enquired Ted.

"I think we've seen the last of him," replied Liz.

Two days later, Jimmy was back on the phone booking another session, better prepared, with six square inches of sticking plaster and paisley pyjama bottoms under his trousers.

"How did your man go?" asked Ted.

"I think we've got him for life," said Liz.

At 31, Jimmy Hill had tasted riding, was happy to be a "horsaholic" and had bought a comfortable pair of jodhpurs. A few months after his first lesson, daily hacking and jumping sessions, the Edgars told him he was going hunting — a sport this townie had only previously seen on Christmas cards.

They gave him a horse, a hat, boots, jacket, tied his stock and he remembers: "I stuck like glue to the Edgars, because my fear of being an idiot, lost and alone in the countryside, was greater than my fear of the fences."

That day with the North Warwickshire was to lead to 20 years of foxhunting, sugarless tea to keep his weight down and an unforgettable partnership with his fourth horse, the noble and rugged Buchan. The horse was bought in 1976 from Ted Edgar's friend David Tatlow for £2,000, and had been named after Martin Buchan, Manchester United's number six, because David was a fan.

Jimmy, however, nicknamed the six-year-old Irish chesnut gelding "Spotty Bottom", because he looked as if someone had splashed white paint on his quarters.

"Spotty Bottom said he was the boss, and I said that was OK by me," declares Jimmy. "He would jump anything and once he had made up his mind, you could forget trying to brake and just prepare yourself for the leap."

executive TV role, also appearing on the small screen.

He fronted *Match of the Day* for 15 years and is now the expert Desmond Lynam turns to for no-punches-pulled commentary.

This amiable 67-year-old grandfather, who now lives in two 16th century Sussex cottages knocked together, with bits added on, is also chairman of Fulham Football Club. But the first thing visitors see when they enter his home is not football memorabilia, but a pastel portrait of Buchan hanging in the hall.

This revered horse was one of the reasons Jimmy Hill moved to Gloucestershire in the 1970s to a house with stables, so that Buchan could be at home. The horse gave as much warmth to his humans as a good malt whisky and a log fire on a winter's night.

Jimmy loved not only his horse but his sport, too: "As an ignoramus, I was unaware of hunting's refinements, but was concerned with the thrill of the chase and what got between you and what you were after. Dear Buchan would tackle anything. Out with the Heythrop, they would say, 'Here he comes' and give us a little space because of the problem with brakes."

They jumped everything, even people who accidentally got in the way, including a racehorse trainer prone in a ditch and one of Prince Charles's friends in a heap the other side of a hedge, which earned Jimmy a dressing down from the girl's mother.

Buchan and Jimmy had 13 years together until Jimmy's back trouble flared and he was in spasm for nearly a year. He could not bear to sell Buchan, so gave him to friends Richard and Penny Tetley to hunt, while Jimmy paid visits bearing edible gifts.

"I remember I hadn't seen him for a while and as I walked into the Tetley's yard, he immediately pricked up his ears and put his head over the door because he recognised my voice."

Buchan was ailing and in his 20s when the Tetleys telephoned Jimmy to say it would be best if the horse was put down.

"We were in tears at both ends of the phone," says Jimmy sadly. "That horse was wonderful to me. He was kind in the stable and a brilliant hunter. He was a giver of pure pleasure."

26 October 1995

The worst Buchan ever did was to strike out and break Jimmy's daughter's elbow when she was hacking out on her pony with her father. A ghastly act made worse because it was Joanna's first ride after breaking a leg show jumping.

"The pony upset Buchan," Jimmy protests.

But he made up for it when Captain Brian Fanshawe invited Jimmy and Buchan to ride upsides as he hunted the Cottesmore's hounds.

"The Captain was a wonderful rider, jumping everything from a stride. He just turned and popped. Buchan did not let me down — I think it was his family pride."

There had been no longing for a pony as a boy, nor even a football. It was not until Jimmy played in an Army match that soccer was considered a career.

The bearded Jimmy, who shaved the famous chin for £3,000 at a charity auction, was a rare commodity -— an articulate footballer. He was chairman of the Professional Footballers' Association and, after his playing and managing days were over, moved smoothly into an

The "agony aunt" who enjoyed making mischief

Chairman of the British Dressage Supporters Group Desi
Dillingham recalls her sensational partnership with Marcus, a horse
with a few tricks up his sleeve whose spirit hunts on forever

THEY say a dog answers you, while a cat takes a message and gets back to you. But a horse ...? Well, a horse called Marcus became an agony aunt.

"When you are a teenager," says Desi Dillingham, "there are times when the rest of the world does not understand you.

"Boy!" she exclaims in her Canadian accent, "did I tell Marcus all about it. If I had a fight with my family, I would lie down with him, my head on his neck, tell him of my woes and problems and he would understand. Marcus was my best friend."

It all sounds sweetness and light, but Marcus and Desi, the 100 megawatt personality who is currently orchestrating Olympia's 1995 British Equestrian Olympic Fund extravaganza, were the scourge of the Canadian equestrian scene. When the Dillingham lorry pulled in, the hearts of other competitors sank because they knew they had lost their class before they had entered the ring.

She and Marcus were leading show jumpers, eventers, working hunters, and the partnership waltzed away with hack and equitation classes.

Desi, christened Leslie, was the eldest daughter of Franklin Dillingham, Field Master of the Lake of Two Mountains Hunt, and his wife Pam, director of the Montreal Horsemanship Club and senator of the Canadian Olympic three-day event team.

Marcus was their home-bred white-faced 16.1hh bay gelding, a $\frac{3}{4}$ Thoroughbred who was handed down to Desi when he was seven and she was 12, and already 5ft 8ins and capable of show jumping her own height as easily as her peers would pop open a packet of sweets.

A year to Desi then was only seven months long, beginning in May when the curtain opened on the spring shows and ending in November when the winter snows closed the short hunting season.

At 14, she won the intermediate section of the Ottawa Valley three-day event, limping off crutches with cartilage trouble to hop on Marcus, and then went on to take the Orstown Fair indoor junior show jumping championship with fences at 5ft 2in.

They do not pussyfoot around in Canada, says Desi Dillingham. When course-builders erect fences, they generally need stepladders.

At 15 and under age, she needed written permission from the Canadian horse trials authority to compete at advanced level with Marcus in the Eastern Championship at Senneville. They did not win, but caused a sensation for their fluent performance. A year later, Desi won a steeplechase with him.

"The most exciting ride of my life," says the proud jockey.

The solid silver platter from the last sortie is now in the living room of her handsome north London flat overlooking Little Venice, while the rest of her riding memorabilia is on the old family farm in Quebec, where her 78-year-old mother still lives and who she will be joining for Christmas.

Few in Britain see Desi as a former rider so proficient that she was judged in an equitation class to have a superior seat to that of Ian Miller, the Canadian show jumper who twice won the World Cup.

Here, she is "dynamo Desi", now in her sixth and last year as chairman of the British Dressage Supporters Group, member of the BHS Dressage Group's main committee, who has helped raise thousands of pounds and the sport's profile, staged the Volvo World Cup qualifier at Wembley and is about to put the final gloss on Olympia's gala night on 14 December.

This 48-year-old Porsche-driving bachelor girl, who founded and runs the Masterlock Recruitment company, came to England when she was 25, leaving behind the horse who meant most to her.

Desi recalls: "He was difficult to hack out because he shied at everything, but in competition, when the chips were down, he was always spot on, with manners to burn.

"He liked lying down in his stall, but he never got straight to his feet like other horses. He sat up first on his haunches like a dog."

Marcus also had a couple of cute tricks. He would gently take a sugar cube from between Desi's lips and answer the snap of her fingers with a rude gesture.

Once, when her mother was showing members of the Spanish Riding School around their yard, Desi said to Marcus, surreptitiously snapping her fingers: "What do you think of these people, Marcus?" On cue, he poked out his tongue.

Desi's partnership with Marcus, the gamest of all her horses, ended bitterly when his penchant for escaping from the stable proved his undoing. Galloping through flowers and vegetable beds

was not an unusual occurrence. But the gardener who caught him that last fateful time, put him back in his stable, forgetting that the shovel was still against the wall. Marcus turned and sliced open his leg to the tendons.

He was in shock, got colic and Desi and her mother tearfully sat up nursing him through the night.

"He recovered from the colic," she said. "I kept hoping he would come sound. But it slowly dawned on me that it would never be right."

Desi Dillingham did not consider a career in riding and certainly not one in dressage — which in

those days was only to be endured for the sake of competing in a three-day event. She went to business school, while Marcus was retired on the farm.

By the time Marcus was put down in his late 20s, Desi was an established career woman in Britain.

"I couldn't be heartbroken," she said candidly, "because any animal we have ever owned has always been given the most magnificent life. I was always taught as a child that when horses died they went to the hounds and their spirit hunted on forever. They went with honour and without fear.

"I wish when my time comes that I could be dispatched with such kindness and that my spirit could hunt on forever."

2 November 1995

The Monarch who reigned in so many spheres

Anneli Drummond-Hay recalls the colourful and sometimes controversial career of the most versatile horse

FRED WINTER wanted to ride him in the Grand National, Gunner Andersson thought him perfect for pure dressage, Bill Steinkraus desired him for show jumping, and Lars Sederholm, who at the last count has had 7,000 horses through his training centre, says he was the best horse he has ever seen.

"Just fantastic."

Merely-A-Monarch, an equine Jack of all trades, was the master of them all.

In the space of one 12-month period, he won Burghley, three dressage classes in a row, left a racehorse called Flame Gun in his slipstream on private gallops, won Badminton and, two months later, came out as a show jumper at the White City, sweeping away the Imperial Cup from the big boys at his first international show.

So what made Merely-A-Monarch multi-talented.

"He was a freak," Anneli Drummond-Hay says, without a second's hesitation. She also points out, however, that the handsome 16.3hh nearly black horse with a distinctive blaze was an extravagant mover, blessed with excellent conformation and cursed by a wicked buck, which could unseat her without regard for place or occasion.

He could buck her off while hacking or receiving a rosette and gallop away.

"I lived in fear of finding him smashed by a car," she says.

The mighty Monarch was cheeky, powerful, sometimes an outrageous hooligan, occasionally ungenerous and always a first-class cuddle in the stable.

Anneli rode him with a neckstrap and, looking back, the only time he gave a buck which could have been worthy of an affectionate pat on the neck was when he rocketed the top South African show jumper Errol Wucherphennig over his neatly clipped ears.

Anneli is the former Mrs Wucherphennig.

Most of the time, Anneli adored the gelding, but their first years together were quarrelsome.

"The domestic rows were endless," she recalls, "and I had a lot of serious talks with him."

Anneli was 21 when she found Monarch through a wanted advertisement in *Horse & Hound*. She was not entirely captivated by his breeding, because she had already owned a horrible horse by Happy Monarch, but she could not ignore how this three-year-old filled the photograph sent by the vendor.

She bought him for £300 and later refused a £60,000 offer for him.

"I had my whole life wrapped up in this horse," explains Anneli, "and did not sell because I believed we were meant to stay together. Although I desperately needed the money, the career I thought the two of us could have together was more important."

The career was indeed hallmarked nine carat gold, with a spicy front page involving Monarch's "kidnap".

It is a lengthy tale which began with Anneli striking a £7,000 deal with the father of one of the richest, most powerful and famous businessmen in Britain today. The father would own the horse. but Anneli would always have the ride.

It was at the time that Monarch was putting in a few stops and his lady jockey was being blamed. It was the time, too, when Monarch, without her, was on the short-list for the 1964 Olympics.

One night, while Anneli was asleep at her Oxfordshire stables, Merely-A-Monarch was quietly spirited away and offered to David Broome, who innocently accepted the ride. Anneli fought for Monarch in court, got him back and had to return the £7,000.

Anneli, now 58, was speaking from Antwerp, where she is based with three horses before competing on the European indoor circuit with the ultimate aim of representing South Africa at Atlanta. She remembers the saga as if it happened yesterday.

There were tears, the horse not going well for David, how Col Tom Greenhalgh gave her the money to get him back, and the discovery of an abscess, which she believes caused Monarch pain and to falter in front of fences.

She said: "They wanted the best horse for the Olympics and the best rider. David Broome was on top and the horse was dreadful. David said afterwards it was the stupidest thing he had ever done."

Added Anneli: "I was told if I did not pay for the horse in 30 days it was going to be shot."

The public drama only temporarily blotted their show jumping copybook. At home, between 1962 and 1970, they won seven Area International Trials, three national championships and the Queen Elizabeth II Cup.

Abroad, they chalked up four Nations Cup team wins, eight Grands Prix, six championships and three puissance classes. Anneli was leading lady rider at 13 international shows and holds the record for winning six competitions in six days at Geneva.

She retired Merely-A-Monarch in 1972, when she married and set off for a new life in Johannesburg, where she became a leading rider on the South African circuit.

Monarch enjoyed a happy-ever-after retirement in the care of Merlin Meakin, who had been Anneli's groom for 10 years and Monarch's devoted slave.

Whereas Anneli could see the horse's faults, Merlin considered him faultless and worshipped him.

At an overseas show, when Anneli was eliminated from a Grand Prix for missing out a fence, Merlin furiously reprimanded her for letting down Monarch.

Merlin took Monarch hunting and on one occasion she was surprised when a chap dismounted at a covert, raised his top hat and announced solemnly and soberly: "Excusé me, but I really must kiss the great Merely-A-Monarch."

Merely-A-Monarch, the spirited king, was put down after collapsing when he was around 25. By chance, Anneli Drummond-Hay was visiting Britain at the time and she says softly: "It was almost as though he waited for me to say goodbye."

9 November 1995

The most explosive Rolls Royce of them all

Sending for Ron Barry was the solution when desperate measures were considered for a desperate horse

THEY sent especially to the north for "Big Ron" because a desperate horse needed a desperate measure.

The Dikler had already scattered a point-to-point crowd, been expelled like a delinquent schoolboy from one reputable training establishment and carted Stan Mellor, who had been enjoying an unassailable lead, straight on into Lingfield racecourse's car park, instead of obligingly going left-handed at the bend and waiting patiently for the post.

In his second training yard, The Dikler, renowned for his scatterbrain ways, sulks and diabolical blunders, was equally mean, but tolerated because of his undoubted talent, which never saw him fall.

Only his silken-handed lad Darkie Deacon could cope with him and the boss Fulke Walwyn knew that if Darkie was off sick, he would come down in the morning and find the rest of the staff had rapidly scattered to the furthest corners of the premises. No one wanted to be saddled with the devil called The Dikler.

The horse revelled in his perfect pace, which was "bolt", excelled at rearing and in his chosen demeanour, which was ferocity.

When The Dikler's previous racing partners Willie Robinson and Barry Brogan had hung up their boots, Terry Biddlecombe told Fulke Walwyn of Ron Barry, a wild Irishman from the north with a reputation for riding horses others feared and for also chatting and telling jokes non-stop throughout all his races.

The legend goes that sometimes the punchlines

were delivered in the ambulance, weighing room or even during the next race. Ron Barry could give the worst horses the best rides, and other jockeys a headache.

Ron travelled south to Lambourn from Pooley Bridge overlooking Lake Ullswater and mounted The Dikler for two practice fences, with the more religious in the yard discreetly crossing themselves.

"The Dikler was massive. Huge. I had never sat on such a powerful horse before," recalls Ron. "The ride lasted two seconds. He ran away, jumped the fences and pulled himself up, and somewhere in between I wondered whether he would stop in Berkshire or carry me back to Cumbria."

Four days later, Limerick-born Ron Barry and the tearaway equine known as the *enfant terrible* of British steeplechasing won the 1973 Cheltenham Gold Cup by a short head from Pendil at odds of 9-1.

"It was a terrific spare ride," declared Ron, "and I was elated. The horse clearly had a terrible mind of his own at home, but was not so bad on the track.

"There was always a battle in races where there were only two or three runners and we had to come to a little arrangement.

"He wanted to put his head down and go, and I had to use brute strength to hold him. We had a fight and then he would settle. His power was unbelievable."

Ron partnered The Dikler when the horse was 10 and rode him for the next three years before he was retired. They were second in their next Cheltenham Gold Cup, won the Whitbread Gold Cup at Sandown after an objection and twice superbly jumped round the Grand National, only running out of petrol in the last half mile.

"He was a jockey's dream, popping the Chair like a hurdle."

Ron Barry became champion jump jockey twice and, today, is still based at his Pooley Bridge smallholding, but now works as the Jockey Club inspector of the 24 northern courses. His other business, run by his wife Liz, entails building kennels and loose boxes for such as Jodami.

In his heyday, he was known as King of the Chat and admired for his courage, and, of his 850 winners, Ron Barry reckons The Dikler was "the kinkiest and most explosive Rolls Royce of them all."

The Dikler's owner Peggy August, who became Mrs Boddington, thought The Dikler was originally worth next to nothing.

Her uncle Edward Bee bought the 17.1hh bright bay gelding by Vulgan in Ireland subject to the vet but, sadly, Mr Bee died the morning the vet telephoned to say the horse had passed the examination.

The steely vendor insisted the deal went ahead and Mrs Boddington was forced to bring the horse to England.

"He is not worth twopence," said Mrs Boddington, who, now stuck with the horse, nicknamed him Twopenny, had him broken and rode him around the lanes herself. She later sent him into his first training establishment, only to find him back on her doorstep again because of his unruly behaviour.

Today, Mrs Boddington, of Burford, Oxfordshire says: "Twopenny was perfectly behaved at home,

sparkling at everything he was asked to do. It was only training, with 20lbs of oats going to his head which turned him from Dr Jekyll into Mr Hyde."

The Dikler won two point-to-points, the working hunter at Thame show, 14 steeplechases, was second seven times and third six times. When he retired from the track, having run in a record seven Gold Cups, Mrs Boddington's step-daughter Jackie hunted him and rode him in riding club activities.

He was put down when he was 22, having spent the last year nannying young stock at Signet Hill Farm.

"We were heartbroken when he died," Mrs Boddington told me.

"He was a brilliant horse," added Ron Barry.

16 November 1995

The clown who became a Big Top attraction

Mary Chipperfield recalls the dazzling career of Pedro, the
Andalusian horse who won a gold medal in the circus "Olympics"

I N the same showy way drivers cruise their custom cars around London's Chelsea on the final Saturday night of the month, the riders of southern Spain bring out their best horses for a flamboyant sherry-laden festival.

Watching the dazzling annual equine spectacle in Jerez's glittering sun was Mary Chipperfield, the seventh generation circus artiste, who was captivated by the powerful Andalusian stallions.

A further trip to a Majorcan stud resulted in the purchase of Pedro, a fiery £300 yearling colt, who was loaded on to a potato boat for a further £300 fare, including delivery to Dover.

Now aged 29, the horse is fat and as fit as a fiddle. He amuses himself by bossing five llamas in his field and, with his ears laid back and teeth bared, he chases cars if they dare to encroach on the driveway on the other side of his personal hedge.

In his time, Pedro the 16.1hh grey is reputed to have executed the best piaffe and passage in Britain, while Mary Chipperfield, who trained him, could easily have been an Olympic dressage rider.

She ignored the plea of the establishment, turned a deaf ear to Col Harry Llewellyn's exhortations to give up the circus and concentrate on pure dressage, and chose instead to follow family tradition and stay in the confines of the 12m diameter sawdust ring.

International trainer Sylvia Stanier reckons Pedro is among the best and likens him to Burmese, the horse the Queen rode in rehearsals for Trooping the Colour.

Both horses were all bounce and charisma, but the moment the bands played they buckled down to work like true professionals. In fact, Sylvia thought so much of Pedro that she once travelled to Switzerland to give him his favourite English apples.

Mary is not surprised that the Andalusian has engendered such respect and affection, for her own relationship with him has surpassed all her other experiences in a lifetime spent with a variety of animals. She has worked with lions, llamas, elephants and Liberty horses — and even a tiger.

Mary and Pedro achieved a gold medal in their own sphere, the circus "Olympics" at Monte Carlo, where in a competition watched by Monaco's royalty and diamond-clad glitterati, they won the world championship for circus high school, which contains all the dressage movements plus the extravagant Big Top extras such as the Spanish walk and the polka.

Pedro is better known than you might think. He was Paul Daniel's vanishing horse on television, the horse on whom Princess Michael learned to ride side-saddle and is used in Sylvia Stanier's best-selling equestrian book, *The Art of Long Reining*. On pages 38 and 39 he demonstrates leg yields and on page 42 he is captured performing piaffe.

"He is the most talented horse," says Mary, "and I have had such a rapport with him. All I needed to do was twitch a muscle or two and he would say: 'Oh yes, she is asking me to do passage'.

"He loves people and performing. In Monte Carlo he knew it was a big occasion and rose to it. He worked better than ever. As for travelling, you

could put him anywhere with anything — camels, llamas ..."

Mary, a 5ft 4in tousle-haired blonde, is the daughter of the late Jimmy Chipperfield, the circus boss who brought safari parks to Britain. She was educated at boarding school where she learned to ride and continued riding after leaving by joining the Massarellas for a year.

She show jumped at White City, hunter trialled and point-to-pointed and went on to become a dressage pupil of Freddie Knie and the Olympic trainer Georg Wahl.

Pedro was bought as a pleasure horse, something handsome to ride. At seven, though, he turned into a star workhorse, while his elegant rider wore sequinned costumes from Paris. They performed all over Europe four times and around Britain twice, the continental audiences giving them ecstatic applause, particularly the Germans, while the British seemed harder to please.

Mary, now 57, and married to Roger Cawley with two grown-up children, retired Pedro from public life two years ago because the melanomas around his tail became unsightly.

"They don't bother him and I could still pull him out of his field and put him through his paces.

"My only deep regret was that by the time we thought of breeding from him, he was too old and could not remember what he was supposed to do."

Pedro has a winter paddock with a field shelter, and fresh summer pasture to be shared with a larger than life-size equine statue overlooking the Cawley's home in Over Wallop, Hampshire.

Circus training goes on as usual on the 115 acres.

Inside, much of the furniture is being recovered after a tiger cub outgrew its welcome, and outside, the stables contain every sort of quadruped from a zebra to a Shetland pony.

Mary now rides two Portuguese high school horses, about whom she says: "They are good, but the job does not feel the same without Pedro. He's a horse in a million and utterly irreplaceable."

23 November 1995

The bargain that became the dream come true

Ex-footballer and trainer Mick Channon's best horse Piccolo
was straightforward, kind and uncompromising, a real
gentleman who was one of the fastest horses in Europe

A S far as dressing downs in changing
rooms go, this one at Southampton, with
no goals at half-time, lives on in the annals of
soccer history.

Manager Lawrie McMenemy, breathing fire and
heaving a brimstone tongue, lashed his striker
Mick Channon. It lasted three minutes and much
was personal.

As the flames subsided, Channon, flying professional with 308 League goals and 21 for England, politely and calmly enquired: "Have you finished?"

McMenemy nodded.

Channon said wearily: "How many more times have I got to tell you? — football is only my hobby."

It was a useful "hobby", because it paid for the golden-booted Channon's serious endeavour, which was breeding Thoroughbreds.

He studied pedigrees and form and built the Jamesmead Farm Stud on 45 acres near Winchester, Hants. Out of it came the Hennessy Gold Cup and Tote Gold Trophy winners, Ghofar and Jamesmead.

At 38, Channon could have swept into soccer management but, instead, knocked on the Jockey Club door asking for a trainer's license. They turned him down and he imagined he could hear guffaws over his temerity.

However, his second application was granted and, today, at 45, with legs blighted by arthritis and his desperate feet killing him, Channon trains in Lambourn with 100 boxes split between Kingsdown and Saxon Gate.

Mick Channon is speaking fact, for his attitude in both sports has only been businesslike.

With the exception, that is, of Piccolo, whom he has roared past the post. The horse who found a chink in the trainer's armour has been as joyful to him as a winning Lottery ticket.

The 16hh bay colt costing £18,000 raced 21 times between May 1993 and July 1995, won £269,488 and was sold to stud for £500,000.

It is not so much the money, but Piccolo's temperament and the way he ran which arouses Mick's emotions.

"I see myself in him," he says. "He's straightforward, kind, tough, uncompromising, wants to get on with his work and not be fussed over."

Piccolo, by the unfashionable sire Warning, was bashful as a two-year-old, twice not wanting to leave the stalls until the others had gone. The third time, he got smacked on the quarters, which made him rear and start late again.

He had won twice by the time Mick Channon went to York as a 43-year-old for the Keeneland Nunthorpe Stakes. He won it in the Stewards room after Blue Siren was disqualified, and that is when the talk started, raising Mick Channon's hackles.

It was said that Piccolo was not a genuine Group One horse, but the trainer declares loyally: "He did nothing wrong. Piccolo finished in front of Lochsong a few times."

"I suddenly discovered", he was reported as saying at the time, "just how bitchy some people in racing can be."

Which is why Mick Channon's pulse went up the scale in June 1995, as Piccolo flew out of the stalls for the King's Stand Stakes at Ascot. It was a five furlong Group Two race with hot competition, and Piccolo was carrying the Group One penalty.

"He took it up in the final furlong," says Mick, "went away and won easily by $1\frac{1}{2}$ lengths. It was only a fraction outside a track record. And he proved that he was a top-class horse."

Then, two days before the Sussex Stakes at Goodwood, Piccolo was walking home after working on the gallops, when he suddenly went lame.

"I was behind him in the Land Rover," says Mick, "and he was hopping."

Mick Channon could have said that he was as sick as a parrot when Piccolo was examined and found to have a fracture of the pastern.

Mick instead remarks: "I was so disappointed. I haven't had many as good as him."

The injury caused consternation among two of Piccolo's greatest fans, his lad Laurence Spong and Laurence's young daughter Chloe.

"I was so numb when it happened," confesses Laurence. "I was expecting the worst and just sat down and cried. He was the be all and end all of my life for two years, and I hated seeing one of the fastest horses in Europe having to stand in his stable getting bored.

"Piccolo is a real gentleman, the quietest of colts. Chloe adores him and comes into the box to stroke him. He's so good with her, she can walk underneath him and he doesn't mind."

Laurence says: "I'll be gutted when he goes to stud, but glad to know he's going to have a great life."

Mick adds: "This horse only gave satisfaction. It was satisfying to see him run and prove the critics wrong. He was the bargain that became the dream come true."

30 November 1995

The Pink Pig who flew fearlessly over fences

Amateur huntsman Nigel Peel recalls 10 glorious seasons with the bold, brave little horse who only ever wanted to stay with hounds

TWO words were used to describe the horse being sold over the telephone to Nigel Peel. "Ugly" and "brilliant".

"And by the way," said Nigel's cousin, enthusiastically, as if it might clinch the deal, "it is the colour of a Simmental cow."

Nigel reluctantly agreed to try the horse in a collecting ring at the Royal Show, where he was stewarding and, there, amid a flurry of elegant show hunters, stood an embarrassing excuse for a horse, one more suited to a cowboy and indian B movie than to a Master of Foxhounds, huntsman and National Light Horse Breeding Society (HIS) judge.

Nigel Peel is not a strange man, indeed, generally he is considered to have sound opinions and exquisite taste, but he took a look at the 15.2hh cob called Mr Whippy and admits unabashedly that he instantly fell in love. And, after popping him over a fence, decided that the horse was "absolute heaven".

He renamed the four-year-old, Geronimo, and sent him home on a cattle float to Devon where Miss Daisy Carne-Williams, a former Master of the Taunton Vale, viewed the £450 purchase and exclaimed: "You have bought THAT? Good God. It is a bloody great pink pig."

Thereafter, ex Mr Whippy, ex Geronimo, became the Pink Pig, a sturdily framed horse with a fine shoulder, who was never sick or lame, rode like a 16.2hh and jumped fearlessly for 10 seasons, first in Taunton Vale country and then with the Chiddingfold, Leconfield and Cowdray.

The brightly-coloured, hog-maned package came with good points and some fear-provoking bad ones. He viewed his occupation as one of staying with hounds, whether Nigel agreed with him or not, and, as far as the Pink Pig was concerned, all gates were solidly locked, could not be opened and consequently needed jumping.

No amount of discussion could persuade him otherwise, and as Nigel recalls: "It made coming home at night extremely hairy."

The horse once cracked Nigel's collar-bone during one of their interminable rows at a gate, and was only prepared to stand quietly at a meet for 10 minutes precisely. This required Nigel to gulp his stirrup cup, give instructions and hear gossip before the Pink Pig began unsociably to walk on his hind legs.

On the credit side, though, the Pink Pig would be a marvel when Nigel Peel dismounted and abandoned him to plunge into thick undergrowth on a hot morning's cubhunting to ensure hounds were drawing properly.

No matter how far Nigel travelled unseen on foot, how circuitous the route, and the length of time, the Pink Pig was always placidly waiting at the exit.

"I never knew whether he jumped anything to get to me," says Nigel, "but he was always there without fail."

Nigel Peel was born to hunt. School was purgatory, six months with a stockbroker were disastrous and happiness was when he was invited to be an amateur whip with the Cowdray.

At 20, he became Joint-Master and huntsman of the Goathland in North Yorkshire. He was there two years, spent three with the Cambridgeshire, another three with the Taunton Vale, moved to his home Hunt, the Chiddingfold, for the next nine seasons and is now the 44-year-old huntsman of the North Cotswold, sharing the Joint-Mastership with his wife Sophia.

In his diary, under 14 September, 1977, he wrote of his first morning's hunting with the Pink Pig: "Took to it like a duck to water."

Another entry says: "Boldest and bravest horse of my life." This followed a fearful ride in fading

light when Nigel thought he might face losing a pack of flying hounds. Peel and the Pig were faced by two strands of 3ft 6in wire, a ditch and a towering hedge.

"I don't want it to sound like a fisherman's tale, but it was enormous, and as I turned the little horse to jump it, I said to myself: 'This might be the most stupid thing I have ever done in my life.'

The Pink Pig soared over, and the drop was as great the other side."

There was another terrific hunt over the Leconfield estate, 12 miles as hounds ran, when, towards the end of the day, at almost racing pace, Peel and the Pig jumped some appalling drop fences at Limba Farm.

"It was deep Sussex going and I was hanging on the end of the buckle," says the huntsman. "The Pink Pig was such a star. What that horse wanted was to stay with hounds. He never tired and never gave up, once running 90 minutes without a check, and nothing was too big for him to jump. He hated being interfered with and as long as I sat still, we got on frightfully well."

The Pink Pig's painting hangs in the Peels' farmhouse at Stow-on-the-Wold, Gloucestershire, where Nigel described how the horse, in his ninth season, stopped for the first time in front of a fence. With a sinking heart Nigel knew the writing was on the wall, for, at 15, the little horse was clearly growing tired.

They shared their last day of a decade together on 12 December, 1987 when the huntsman gave the gallant Pig to his chum Stan Mayes to enjoy more gentle times with hounds. Nigel's son Jamie, who was six, was puzzled and asked Stan. "Why have you got Daddy's horse?"

He replied: "Because your father wants the horse to go to heaven without the inconvenience of dying."

The Pink Pig was put down before cancer caused him any prolonged suffering, and Nigel Peel says today: "If I was told I had to gallop at the River Styx and if I cleared it I would go to heaven, and, if not, I would go to hell, I would choose to sit on the Pink Pig. He was something special and exceptionally clever.

"He could have jumped into a paper bag without tearing it."

7 December 1995

The unwanted horse who became a hero

Malcolm Pyrah recalls his nine-year partnership with Anglezarke and the electric relationship which won the team every honour imaginable

THE way his front legs whirled like a windmill in a gale, the horse could have been Dutch. Instead, he was born in Ireland and few wanted him, particularly Malcolm Pyrah.

"Do not buy him," he warned the late Thomas Hunnable of Towerlands Equestrian Centre, but Anglezarke, a chesnut gelding named after a Lancashire moor, was part of the arrangement devised by dealer Trevor Banks.

If Hunnable, a celebrated patron of the sport, and Pyrah, his chosen jockey, wanted Bank's great horse Chainbridge, then Anglezarke had to be part of the package, securely wrapped.

Anglezarke's price alone was £60,000 on a sale or return basis - £30,000 down and the rest in six months' time. At most, it was going to be money on the muck heap, or at least a wasted, tortuous half year.

The pair of horses arrived at Malcolm's Keyworth Farm in Nottingham in 1980 – Chainbridge to a red carpet welcome, while Anglezarke, a tense nine-year-old, did not even merit a pat.

"I hated him," said Malcolm, "and I hated the ride. He was awful and could not even canter in a straight line."

Then a minor miracle happened. Malcolm and Anglezarke connected as though the rider had supercharged the horse's dead battery with exactly the right jump leads. The antagonists were then sweetly purring in unison, just like a highly effective engine.

At the end of their first three weeks together they picked up a championship at the Norfolk show and were Wembley-bound, where, as rank outsiders, Malcolm and Towerlands Anglezarke won the title of Leading Show Jumper of the Year.

"No one expected it of us, so it was quite a buzz," said Malcolm.

There was more electricity to come in the next nine years – a European individual silver medal, another one in the World Championships, two European team gold medals, eight Nations Cup team wins, and a sixth place in the team at the 1988 Seoul Olympics. Winnings totalled £349,426 and still Malcolm had no love for him. "There was respect instead. It was a partnership," he said.

Horse and rider were similar in the way they both had their careers interrupted. Malcolm's interruption came during a sojourn in local government where he pushed school meals around on paper, neatly filing them away in a cabinet in a local education department. Anglezarke's happened as a youngster when his star potential plummeted to earth.

Malcolm had always been a serious rider, even as a boy in gymkhana classes with a string of ponies, and expected to win more than an average working man's weekly wage on a summer weekend. At the age of 17 until 23, he donned a suit to work at Hull Town Hall until he sensibly quit and went to Trevor Banks. Two years later he was competing nationally and moved on to John Massarella's yard. At 32, he married show jumper Judy Boulter and they set up their own horse

Anglezarke went to Trevor Bank's yard where Michael Saywell was the jockey. Malcolm does not mince his words: "The combination did not click and Anglezarke fell from favour like a lead balloon."

At Keyworth Farm, the gelding had a new lease of life. "He needed routine to flourish. He had to be ridden first thing in the morning, groomed and then he would lie down for as long as you let him. He conserved his energy for the job as the best horses always do. The 'system' here suited him. He relaxed and became a new horse to ride."

Malcolm soon learned Anglezarke's quirks. You could not turn him sharp right-handed into a fence, but there was no problem with the left, and he had to be kept well off a vertical. But his Achilles' heel was water – and this, believes Malcolm, prevented the horse from achieving Milton's successes.

Maddeningly, one of the few times he jumped water determinedly was when he was supposed to walk quietly through it out hunting with Judy. "He never made any effort," complained Malcolm. "Yet that one day he was determined he was not going into the water. He cleared 12 feet, shot Judy over the top and dislocated her finger."

Anglezarke retired from show jumping after the gruelling Seoul Olympics, and hunted for three seasons. By then his old legs had become too worn and he was retired completely, with the thought that he would enjoy being pampered.

Sadly Anglezarke did not take gracefully to being an old age pensioner and began to fade. Malcolm came back from a trip one day in 1992 and murmured to his horse: "I cannot leave you like this, old boy."

For a man who professed never to have loved the horse, he acted in a contrary fashion. He asked a friend to hold Anglezarke for the vet and made sure Judy and daughter Nikki were off the premises and oblivious to what was happening. As the horse was put down, Malcolm was far away, walking alone across his fields.

14 December 1995

trading business. At 33, Malcolm began riding regularly for Britain.

Now 54, the articulate Yorkshireman is trainer and *chef d'équipe* to the British Young Riders' team. He still has a full thatch of blond hair and his files are as efficient as they were in his town hall days. Anglezarke's sale agreement, dated 4 June, 1980, is to hand – as is the horse's full story.

The 16.3hh chestnut "dished" so extravagantly that as a three-year-old he remained unsold at a trio of auctions before the hammer went down at £250. He was brought to England and sold for £1,200 to Adrian Marsh, a keen amateur, whose Young Riders' win on him was a sensation at the Horse of the Year Show. He then sold Anglezarke for a sum that enabled him to buy a farm and start up a thriving business.

The very devil of a pony

Olympia's favourite pony, Willum, is reliable, dependable
and unbeatable and, at 23 years old, is fighting fit and as
fast as a bullet

BEHIND the scenes at show jumping's greatest Christmas party, all was not entirely festive sweetness and light. This was because, it has to be said, on the Friday there will have been the usual squabbles, petty jealousies — and even a tussle between the Whitaker brothers.

This was the afternoon when the big boys rode the little ponies in the traditional crowd-pleasing event known as the show jumpers' gymkhana.

The riders' will to win did not evaporate just because there were no fences in the arena. On the contrary, they were just as competitive in the sack race as in any Grand Prix and the trouble started for the simple reason that they all wanted to ride the same pony — Willum.

"You see," says Serena Cornford, daughter of his owner, "they know Willum is the fastest and the best."

Willum has been at every Olympia since 1977 and during that time has carried some of the great names, including Harvey Smith, Robert Smith, David Broome, Michael Whitaker, Nick Skelton and Lesley McNaught.

The grooms also have their own special Olympia Christmas competition, show jumping over a 3ft course. Some of them are allowed to enter the top horses they look after, others have to hunt around for a spare ride, in which case they go searching for reliable, dependable, unbeatable Willum. On countless occasions, this fancy dress and pantomime artiste has snatched the first prize from the equine giants.

Willum is 23 years old, fighting fit and as fast as a bullet. In his professional life, this 13.2hh chestnut pony, with a white star and three white socks, is an angel, with halos piling one on top of another. But in his private life he carries a trident, has horns and a forked tail — the very devil of a pony.

Take his professional life first. At five, he was talent-spotted and invited to join the Enfield Chace branch of the Pony Club's Prince Philip Cup mounted games team. Willum specialises in litter lifters, flag flyers, postman's express, sock and bucket and the mug shuffle.

His *piece de resistance* is bending races, all of which has merited two trips to Wembley.

But he has also won three part-bred Arab performance championships, dressage, cross-country, show jumping and working hunter pony competitions.

This year, his current full-time jockey, 15-year-old Fay Jackson, dreamed of riding at Hickstead, so she joined the BSJA, travelled with Willum to Sussex and came back with both the Junior British Novice and Discovery classes in the bag.

The Cornford family from Hertfordshire have regularly turned down cascades of money for him. Two years ago, when Willum was 21, they were offered £5,000. Ten years ago, the amounts were around £25,000, and one was even a blank cheque.

Serena Cornford's mother, Margaret, was so indignant about the attitude of one rich, flashy parent, who wanted Willum for any price, that she retorted: "I would rather eat him than sell him."

In his private life, says Serena: "Willum is horrid." His major weapon is rearing and boxing anyone who displeases him, particularly those who miss vaulting on him the first time — he does not give them a second chance — or those carrying a syringe, a tooth file or a pair of clippers.

"He undoes bolts, unties knots, loads himself on a lorry, even when you do not want him to, and jumps from field to field. He rounds up other horses, corners them, turns around and kicks them.

"Some years ago, we had a top show Arab as a livery. His owner turned him out, forgetting Willum was out too, then we saw Willum fiercely fence hopping towards the Arab. We ran around screaming, 'Catch the pony', because Willum would have done serious damage to him. He can be such a pig," says Serena.

Margaret Cornford bought Willum, who is by an Arab stallion out of a Dartmoor mare, as a yearling for £150. He went for walks around Hertford town and the surrounding housing estates before being easily broken by her eldest daughter Tanya.

When Tanya grew out of Willum, Serena, today a 30-year-old sales manager, took over the ride. She, too, grew out of him and the Cornfords hunted around for the first in a long line of suitable young jockeys.

Willum is stabled near Serena's home at Bennington in Hertfordshire and only five minutes away from Fay Jackson, who escorted the pony to Olympia this year to put tinsel in his mane and tune him up for the show jumpers.

Fay will be giving Willum a cake on Christmas Day. Her recipe states that you place pasture mix and grated carrot in a bowl, set it in treacle, decorate liberally with mints and pop a carrot in the middle.

Serena says: "Willum has the greatest quality to be found in humans and horses. He always gives his best. He is the most brilliant and generous pony. We cannot imagine life without him."

Nor can Olympia.

21 December 1995

The mare who sailed through testing times

Huntsman Bruce Durno recalls his five blistering seasons with
Samaria, who had the spring of a cat, the cleverness of Einstein
and Houdini's ability to escape

SAMARIA, the chesnut mare, was obviously going to be a useful sort. "If the whipper-in has not got a horse," exclaimed huntsman Bruce Durno dryly, "she is long enough in the back for us both to ride her. She is not a horse, she is a ship."

The mare did indeed move like a stately galleon with a force nine under her tail and leading her into a stable was like docking the QE2. But despite the length between fore and aft, she had the spring of a cat, the cleverness of Einstein and a Houdini-like ability to escape through a bolted door.

One morning, tacked up and rugged, when she was in her first season with Bruce at the Fernie, she tired of waiting for him, so she let herself out

of her stable and yard, ignored the free grazing, and trotted up to his home, popping over a cattle grid on the way.

Bruce was in his bedroom tying his stock. He looked out puzzled, first by the unexpected clatter of hooves, and then by the prevailing silence. "She stood below the window saying: 'Come on, I'm ready, where are you?' "

Bruce Durno, now in his 29th year as huntsman of this fashionable Leicestershire pack with one of the smallest countries on the hunting map, says: "If I had to hunt on forever I would choose 'The Ship'. She always made a day easy for you."

Bruce was born with a silver horn in his mouth at the Heythrop kennels, where his father, Percy Durno, was a huntsman before him. The junior Durno did not require any formal tuition for his chosen sport because, like a sponge, he soaked up knowledge of hounds, horses and hunting from the time he could walk.

At 15, he was second whipper-in to Capt Ronnie Wallace and then first whipper-in at the South Oxfordshire. Even National Service failed to interrupt Bruce's progress, as the Royal Artillery at Oswestry conveniently had their own pack of hounds.

Demobbed in 1958, Bruce became first whipper-in at the Fernie, then kennel-huntsman and finally, in 1966, one of the youngest huntsmen in Britain.

Now 57, he is married with two grown-up children, likes a lot of shooting and a little golf, and is renowned as the "Quiet Huntsman".

This wiry 5ft 9in sportsman was in his floral-papered living room looking through old photographs.

"The Ship", he said, chuckling with genuine fondness, "is not photogenic. When she stood still, she had a habit of dropping her lower lip, hanging out her tongue and laying back her ears. It was not sourness, just her way."

The mare came from show jumper Fred Welch's yard with her breeding unknown but clearly with a dabble of Irish Draught, an indeterminate number of miles on the clock and a licence to thrill.

Liz Powell, 70, who was in charge of the Fernie stables when The Ship arrived in 1969, recalls watching Bruce and the 16.2hh mare sailing across a sea of green.

"You would glimpse them in the distance, trotting easily over a little fence and think, 'Oh, that looks nice and inviting', but when you got up to it you would find a vast ditch in front of the hedge with a post and rails on the other side."

Bruce Durno purses his lips and lets out a "phew", as he recalls Christmas Eve in 1973 when the Fernie met at Lubenham Lodge, home of the late Labour peer, Lord Paget. "You do not get days like that too often," he said.

"We drew one fox and hunted him for four hours and 15 minutes with a 5-mile point and well over 20 miles as hounds ran. She must have jumped between 50 and 60 fences and went without a check for $2\frac{1}{4}$ hours before I managed to change horses.

"The Ship was exceptional. You could jump anything, cut corners where you liked and she only stopped twice for the good reason of saving us from nasty accidents."

There was the time of the heart-stopping magnificent leap from a steep incline, over a big gate, down on to a disused railway line. "I said to her: 'Do not make a mess of this one'."

And another occasion when there was a tortuous jump over a wide cut and laid hedge, straight on to the narrow canal towpath. "That was the sort of thing you could safely do with her," he said with pride. "Any number of horses would have had us in the canal."

Bruce Durno's role requires talented horses. As he says simply: "If you have not got a good horse, you do not get anywhere."

He has used 31 horses down the years as huntsman and almost as many again as whipper-in. He even says there are some better than The Ship, but none held by him in greater affection.

"She had character," he explains. "I could trust her at a Boxing Day meet because she was patent safety with children and I could trust her over 'John Bull country'."

Bruce enjoyed five blistering seasons with The Ship when he reluctantly had to abandon her to less strenuous work and a new home. From there, she hunted on for several more years until heart trouble forced her to drop anchor.

The vet who put her down guestimated her age to be past 20, probably closer to 30. It was the stately Ship's last voyage.

28 December 1995

The star who chose his own friends

Point-to-point jockey and trainer Michael Bloom recalls nine winning years with Skygazer, the single-minded gelding who became a real friend

THE *Timeform* annual stated that the horse "must be tenderly ridden", which was its obscure and genteel way of warning that a whip should never be employed behind Skygazer's saddle. A slap down the shoulder? Yes. On the backside? Absolutely not — and certainly at your own peril.

Unaware of this, jockey Graham MacMillan administered a couple of cracks in the incorrect place after the last fence at Huntingdon, and the horse indignantly bucked and stopped.

Michael Bloom, who knew Skygazer better than anyone, could have told him what would happen, but he was never consulted.

"He was a hands, heels and voice horse," says Michael. "If you hit him he would not race. He would lay his ears back and grunt angrily: 'That's it, get on with it yourself now!'"

Skygazer was bought as a yearling by Noel Arnold, an 80-year-old, one-armed colonel, who sported a magnificent swirling cloak, used a monocular, not binoculars, and once blithely told the Queen Mother they were Norfolk neighbours. He paid £200 for Skygazer and complained that : "That is quite dear enough".

The Colonel wisely placed the tall and lengthy chesnut by Copernicus with the Blooms, a dashing, colourful brigade who were busy rewriting Hunt racing family history — and the record books.

Grandfather Jack Bloom, a farmer and race-rider, came fifth in the Grand National. Son Michael, by way of the Pony Club and show

jumping, entered his first race when he was 15.

Father and son often jousted against each other on the track. Once, having a fiercely quiet discussion at Warwick, father brought son down, each blamed the other, and both wanted to know why the other could not keep his horse on its feet.

Then along came the third generation, Michael's son Nigel, known as "Nibby", and his sister Caroline, and all three Blooms could be seen abreast on the starting line.

Michael remembers Nibby coming up on his inside one day and yelling: "Give me room Dad."

Bloom senior duly and unusually obliged, and had to ride his next 20-plus races with jockeys mocking: "Dad, Dad, give me room."

Now a trainer, Michael rode for 33 years and became the first to score a century in both point-to-pointing and under Rules. He and Nibby are the only father and son combination to win the point-to-point championship.

Although a multitude of horses have passed through Kimberley Home Farm at Wymondham in Norfolk, Michael considers Skygazer alone to be part of the family and a real friend.

He was sweet natured, genuine, trustworthy and the favourite Hunt horse of Michael's wife Jenny. They called the handsome gelding with a floating action "Sky" and broke him in as a three-year-old. He went on to win nine consecutive races and helped Michael clinch the 1969 championship in a death or glory race with the other main contender, Bill Shand Kydd.

It was late in the season at Cottenham and while Shand Kydd on Musk Orchid had other good horses remaining, Michael was rapidly running out of ammunition. Sky went to the front three out, and made a mistake at the open ditch. Musk Orchid swept past and was five lengths in front at the last fence, when Sky surged defiantly ahead to win by a length.

"He was brilliant," says 62-year-old Michael. "The crowd went wild."

They were together for nine years, but then the Colonel died and left Sky to his niece, who removed the horse from the Blooms and sent him to Sir Guy Cunard's yard.

"It broke my heart," says Jenny.

Her husband agrees, declaring: "It was like losing one of the family."

Timeform and the Blooms watched his

progress, but it was clear that, masterminded from new territory, Skygazer's campaign was without distinction.

His successes were credited to the Blooms, as the lazy horse with an electric top gear won eight hunter chases, seven point-to-points and was placed 12 times. This included two fourths with Michael in the Cheltenham Foxhunters, both times on the heavy going the horse detested.

After a bad fall at Wetherby, Skygazer was retired lame from racing as a 15-year-old and was returned home to Norfolk, whinnying with recognition as he came down the ramp.

Michael, who will be opening his 1996 account at Cottenham on 13 January, remembers the long, unsuccessful struggle to try to restore the horse to full health.

"In the end," he says, "we decided the kindest thing would be to put him down. If he could not be happy, it was cruel to keep him alive."

Michael held Sky while the vet dispatched him. He shudders as he remembers: "That was one of the worst days of my life. Nobody spoke in the house for two days after that. If all my horses had all been as kind and genuine as Sky, I would not have broken as many bones."

4 January 1996

The flying devil who became an idol

John Fearnall recalls 22 seasons with his hunter, Willie, who hated humans and horses but loved hounds

J OHN FEARNALL'S seemingly callous words took my breath away.

"I hunted the horse on the Monday and shot him on the Wednesday," he says.

"You sound so cheerful," I protest.

"Ah," he says, "I didn't tell you about Tuesday. I cried so hard in the afternoon that the girl groom thought I was going bananas."

The grief was over a sturdy iron grey called Willie with whom John, a former Field Master of Sir Watkin Williams-Wynn's Hunt, had hunted some glorious 22 years, jumped an estimated 3,000 fences and utterly adored like a devotee of a stone god statue.

It is popularly said among psycho-dynamic counsellors that in a close relationship, one does the loving and one is loved, a conclusion well borne out by John Fearnall and Willie.

Each night for 22 winters, John would check round the stables and stop by Willie's door for a fond chat. On cue, the horse would disdainfully move to the back of the box as if to say grumpily: "What do you want now?".

In the summer, John would walk to the fields where Willie was turned away and the horse would show his back as he headed off in the opposite direction, even if he was offered a bowl of oats. In fact, the only way Willie could be brought up for cubbing was by herding him like a wild mustang.

It was in a mustang's mood that three-year-old Willie arrived in England in 1973, travelling from Co Tipperary. His four equine companions came sweetly down the ramp, while Willie

stayed on board and refused to budge for 36 hours.

It took John Fearnall three months to get to grips with the horse's other oddities, a time span which does not belittle Willie's abhorrence to being ridden, but more amplifies John's determination to stay in the saddle, including one session which lasted from 12.30 to 4.10pm.

During their early days' cubbing, Willie had to be mounted from inside the lorry and for years after, placing a foot in the iron outside a confined space could be a limb-threatening procedure.

So, too, was Willie's dodgem act which could send a proficient foxhunter beagling within four unrideable strides.

John Fearnall would have liked to have sold the horse, even given him away, but he feared this move would damage his horse dealing and hireling business, which numbers Prince Charles among his clientele.

"Bad news about bad horses spreads quickly in the horse world," says John, "so I was forced to keep him and ride him myself. In all my days, I had never come across anything like him."

John Fearnall was blooded when he was three and continued hunting two days a week during school time. John, now 48 and living at the 400-year-old oak panelled Alkrington Hall in Whitchurch, Shropshire, gives a huge belly laugh when he remembers how his crafty headmaster wrought retribution by lining up all 60 pupils of Hanmer village school to catch the truanting John, red-faced and

"That's why he lasted so long," says John, "even though he was only 16.2hh and had to lug my 16 stone. He must have done a minimum of 800 days, including 10 consecutive Mondays, Wednesdays and Saturdays when I was suddenly short of horses.

"He was as hard as nails, did not like people or horses and was utterly brilliant. He only ever showed any affection to hounds."

John recalls a holloa on a Cholmondley Moss woodland when hounds flew for seven miles out of Wynnstay into Cheshire, with Willie neatly cutting corners to stay with the pack, and then later, at Larges during an opening meet, how he fired the horse at a big thorn hedge confidently knowing there would be a dyke behind. But what he had not considered was the farmer digging it out that week with a JCB and putting up a wire oxer.

"We were in mid-air when we spotted it and that old devil just seemed to sprout wings, leap impossibly again and clear it. To this day, I don't know how he managed to do it. He was unbelievable"

Their last hunt was in October 1995 and Willie stayed out until 2.45pm. Later that night, John leaned on his stable door and saw evidence of Willie's kidneys failing and, after confirmation, arranged for the gelding to be put down.

That is when John Fearnall broke with tradition and, instead of sending the horse to the kennels, buried him with honour in a corner of the paddock.

"I know it is all a bit daft," he says, "but the horse was special. If I buy 50 horses a season for the rest of my life, I will never find another like him. Willie and I were mates, even if he did not show it."

11 January 1996

red-handed, en route to a meet at Gredington.

The boy grew up to ride 50 winners point-to-pointing, become a successful farmer with a flourishing horse business and be appointed Field Master in 1977.

Married with two grown-up children, John describes Wynnstay country as the best in England.

"The Quorn," he says mischievously, "go galloping after their tails. We go foxhunting."

It is mostly "close" dairy country with plenty of jumping in which Willie, who was believed to be by King Of Diamonds, was to excel. He never gave more than an inch over an obstacle and never expended unnecessary energy.

The joker who became a pint-sized superstar

Chairman of the Pony Club, Dawn Wofford, recalls her show jumping career with the brilliant "clown", Earlsrath Rambler

THE deal over the Irish horse was hardly convivial, because every time Ralph Blakeway was poised to rise and walk away, telling the vendor the price was too high, his own wife kicked him under the pub table.

Sylvia Blakeway thought the gelding was special, while Ralph considered it yet another uncouth, raw four-year-old.

His opinion merely earned him a further flurry of painful kicks and Ralph said grimly later, he only bought the horse to stop Sylvia breaking his leg.

Her woman's intuition was correct. The bay equine comedian who leapt around like a rubber clown and whose name was Earlsrath Rambler was to become a show jumping superstar and bring the sort of recognition to his rider that top pop singers enjoy today.

Strangers in shops and streets would ask Dawn Palethorpe for her autograph and, when she married, TV cameramen clamoured to be invited to the wedding.

In show jumping's heyday during the 1950s, Dawn and the 15.2hh Earlsrath Rambler helped win around 15 Nations Cups, popped 6ft 6½ins in Puissance, chalked up 16 clear rounds out of 20 at one Horse of the Year Show, and then jumped 190 fences at a string of international shows and only made two mistakes.

Dawn Palethorpe, who, at the tender age of 18, was the leading show jumper of the year in 1954, looks back and pronounces that Earlsrath Rambler, foaled in 1946 of unknown breeding and whose price is lost in the mists of time, was "unique and simply fabulous".

She further adds to the fond praise by declaring: "He was one of nature's very special results."

Today, Dawn Palethorpe is Mrs Warren Wofford, the first woman to be appointed chairman of the Pony Club, who starts 1996 with the challenge of trying to gain independence by breaking away from the BHS, and setting it up as a voluntary youth association.

This 60-year-old grandmother of seven is less daunted by the bid for independence than she was when first presented with Earlsrath Rambler — who became known as Paddy.

The cheeky, strong Paddy was passed to her elder sister Jill, who had the early agony of taking him from novice to Grade A in one brilliant, battling year. The horse did not buck, but leap. He leapt unasked over gates, off roads over hedges, and in the ring, too, at the wrong time in the wrong places.

His *bete noir*, though, was the water jump and the fear he possessed of it was nothing short of rabid. Even years later, when he tolerated such an obstacle, Paddy would enter every arena looking for water, and then raise the question as to whether he would deign to jump it or the fence nearest to it.

This unreliability, coupled with his spookiness in a first class before settling down for the rest of a show, left him and Dawn on the sidelines as reserves for the 1956 Stockholm Games.

In the beginning, his teenage rider from the Palethorpe sausage manufacturing company of Worcestershire, had two tremulous thoughts about Paddy.

She was secretly glad she did not have to contend with his tricks and then, when Jill married and she inherited the ride at 18, she was almost overwhelmed by the responsibility.

"I knew the horse was brilliant, but I worried whether I could do him justice," she says. "Any mistakes would not be his, they would be mine."

Their first success was at Cholmondely Castle, where they divided the open class with Wilf White and Nizefela. It was the start of a whirlwind four years with an excited media trumpeting: "The kid and her pint-sized exuberant horse" who enthralled audiences from Taunton to Toronto.

At the British Army show on the Rhine, Dawn with Paddy and her second horse, Holywell Surprise, won all but one of the international classes. At Aachen, in front of 87,000 people, she picked up the Puissance, the ladies' class and jumped two clear rounds in the Nations Cup.

She and Paddy so impressed supremo Col Mike Ansell that he gave the teenager an open invitation to take Paddy and Holywell Surprise to compete anywhere she wished in the world. They travelled the globe, but at Stockholm Dawn met American Olympic rider and trainer Warren Wofford and thoughts quickly focused on romance. Paddy meanwhile, who had only ever been sweet, registered his disapproval by laying his ears back for the first time ever at the bridegroom to be.

At 22, Dawn took time out to concentrate on being a wife and mother and Paddy was returned to Jill to continue an astonishing record which included carrying both girls for eight consecutive years to places in the Queen Elizabeth II Cup, winning it twice.

In 1963, Paddy suddenly turned into an ordinary, well behaved horse. He stopped leaping and clowning and, while he was still fit enough to compete, Jill decided it was time he should retire. Paddy was 17 and had to be put down when he was 24, reducing the Palethorpe sisters to tears.

"We adored him," says Dawn Wofford. "He was part of our family." She adds feelingly: "It was a privilege to have known him."

18 January 1996

Back to glory for Polly's Pride?

Ladies' point-to-point champion Polly Curling recalls her early
successes with Pastoral Pride, the bonny little horse who,
having had two seasons' rest, is ready for the 1996 campaign

POLLY CURLING, reigning queen of point-to-point riders, split the air with invective when a bay horse arrived in her yard with rain scald and ribs protruding. She said it was smaller than a Labrador and a wreck, only she added an expletive before mentioning the word wreck.

Of no consequence to her was the fact that Pastoral Pride had won over a distance of a mile and a quarter and held a sullied reputation for bolting on gallops.

The three-times national ladies' point-to-point champion was livid over how anyone could allow a horse to deteriorate into such a state and how she would have to nurse it.

Today, eight years later, Pastoral Pride, the horse Polly did not want, has been gifted to her, and their story is double-edged. How the girl, so tough that last year she comfortably beat the men's record, can be reduced to slushy sentimentality over Pastoral Pride, and how the weedy gelding went from nag-to-riches, back to nag-to-rags again, and is currently making a 1996 return to the track.

It took Polly Curling four months to restore the horse to reasonable health, and around 30 minutes to be smitten when she rode him for the first time in November 1988.

"He was such a bonny, butty little horse," she enthuses. "He gave you a wonderful feeling that he would try really hard and loved life."

His *joie de vivre* when he fully recovered could have deterred many other jockeys, but Polly thought him only amusing when he would buck

and bolt on the landing side of a schooling fence.

"Nothing malicious," she says hurriedly. "He does not do anything dirty. He just loves jumping."

Privately, in her Wyndham Lodge yard, between sea and Somerset hills, the equine and his rider became playful.

They had regular games of poke-your-tongue-out and, if horses could laugh, Polly is sure Pastoral Pride would giggle his head off.

Publicly, the pair was about to prove a sensation and leave other horses trailing while they jumped the last fence as the rest of the field were still approaching the one behind them.

The commentator at Windsor would exclaim during one of their races: "And Pastoral Pride's coming to the post and the others are left in the next district."

Pastoral Pride, by Excellor out of Pastoral Miss, came from Ireland as a four-year-old, found by Polly's former boyfriend, who was a jockey for the owners, Chris and Andy Smith, father and son bookmakers.

Polly came via Basingstoke and owes her career to her late stepfather, who had horses in training with Jack Holt. From the age of 11, she was spending school holidays working in the yard and riding out.

Today, the bubbly, photogenic blonde, who has around 150 point-to-point wins and 10 under Rules, is stable jockey to top-of-the-league Richard Barber, but earns her living by breaking and schooling for a variety of clients who include National Hunt trainer Philip Hobbs.

The 15.3hh Pastoral Pride, whom she calls "Josh", and likens to Max Wall for his comic walk when excited, is the horse she has known the longest.

Their first race, at Nedge in Somerset, set the future pattern, with Josh bolting through the field and only settling when he could no longer hear hoof beats behind him. Polly quickly learned that fighting only unbalanced him and, by quietly travelling with him, chalked up a second in only their third race together and won their fourth at 33-1 by more than 40 lengths.

The partnership's next big feature was in 1991, hunter chasing at Fontwell where Josh "made all unchallenged" and finished ahead by around 60 lengths.

The following year, when Josh was seven, Polly reports that he "slammed everything at Warwick, ran a blinder at Windsor and was breathtaking at Cheltenham".

They were in the cavalry charge for the Aintree Foxhunters, where their bid ended in trampled, muddied grief but, while still feeling the bruises, three weeks later hacked up in the £2,162 Taxi News Hunter Chase at Cheltenham.

Polly held her breath while the Smiths refused £18,000 for the gelding and thought she and Josh were set fair for another hunter chasing blitz, but it ended disastrously. They ran three times and pulled up because of Josh's broken blood vessels.

He was turned away and the Smiths decided he should be sent to Martin Pipe for a novice chasing campaign.

"I was crying," admits Polly. "And I could hear the horse bickering as he went off in the trailer, which made it even worse."

She watched him run at Taunton without distinction and in January 1994 she picked up Pastoral Pride and brought him home, a late and much loved Christmas present from the Smiths.

After two seasons' rest, the gelding is fit and ready to run with Polly in the plate at Ludlow on 7 February. She also hopes the man in her life, veterinary surgeon Simon White, will partner Josh in a point-to-point at the end of March.

"To see the two of them coming first past the post would mean more than anything," she declares.

Then she warns: "Josh has come second in six point-to-points, won four hunter chases and two point-to-points. People will not find that impressive, but there are few horses more brave. He is different from any other horse I have known. He is just like a chatty little person."

25 January 1998

The bullfighter who became a classical professor

Author and dressage trainer Sylvia Loch recalls how her stallion
Palomo changed her life and helped turn sport into an art

PALOMO LINARES, wearing a Henry VIII-
style saddle, ornate bridle and ribbons woven
through his mane and tail, majestically carried his
cavaleiro rider and danced with dignity inches
away from the perilous horns in the Portuguese
bullring.

His courage and serenity were rewarded by five
years at stud and then the Persil-white
Lusitano/Arab stallion was pensioned off, only to
appear in public again; this time on the expatriots'
cocktail circuit.

Lady Loch was taking drinks when she was
invited to see him and, in her elegant frock and
unsuitable shoes, trudged across dry, dusty fields.
Palomo's muscle had gone, but there was still a
hint of the old magnificence, enough to entice
Lady Loch into returning the next day to ride
him.

"He was king," she says, "and I felt I was sitting
on a throne. The horse knew everything about
classical dressage and just lifted up his front, sat
down on his hocks and performed."

He cost £1,500 and the Englishwoman who sold
him was glad to see Palomo gone, for her clumsy
novice attempts at riding exploded the horse into
angry levade, sufficient to grace a TV sherry com-
mercial and terrify her.

Lady Loch and Palomo were well matched, as
neither had shirked battle, he in the bullring and
she on paper, when involved in controversy over

the dressage rider's seat. She wrote of her belief in
the great masters' theory of "fork, thigh and seat
bones" making a three-point triangle. Many modern dressage aficionados hotly disagreed and said
that a rider has a two-point seat.

The flurry of furious correspondence did not
stop there because the "them and us" feeling
between Lady Loch, the classical exponent, and
the modern theorists still politely rumbles on.

Palomo signalled part two of her life. This
authoress of the *Royal Horse of Europe*, *The
Classical Seat*, and *The Art of Classical Riding*
laid down her pen and went back to teaching
because she thought the horse was not a
schoolmaster but a professor, not circusey but
correct, the perfect tool in her crusade for clas-
sicism.

Today, Sylvia Loch is celebrating the first
anniversary of her 500-strong Classical Riding
Club, has a full diary of displays and lessons to
be given at home and abroad, and the 16hh
Palomo has a battalion of fans, including one in
the Philippines and one in San Francisco, who
fly to England only for the pleasure of riding
him.

The cast-off bullfighter has starred in a display
at the Royal Mews and won the freestyle dressage
to music competition at the British Association for
the Pure-Bred Spanish Horse Show at Stoneleigh,
four years in succession.

His owner was born Sylvia Cameron and rode wild and free in the Pentland Hills. When she was 24, Sylvia was invited to Portugal and became intrigued by the country's Lusitano horses and high school horsemanship.

To further her equine knowledge and skills, she sought out an academy run by an Englishman, former cavalry instructor, Lord Henry Loch, 29 years her senior.

They married two years later, taught for a decade in the Algarve, and then brought 22 mares and stallions home to Suffolk, where they opened a riding school.

Sadly, Lady Loch was widowed eight weeks after the birth of their daughter Allegra, the school was closed and she turned to writing.

Palomo rearranged her career eight years ago when Sylvia says: "Palomo found me" while she was revisiting friends in Portugal.

She is 50 now, 5ft 10ins, with reddish hair, freckles and a posture which would earn a school deportment badge. She has remarried and is the wife of lawyer Richard Hawkins, living in a Georgian house at Sudbury, where there is an Olympic-sized manege and three other Lusitano companions for the muscle-rippling 23-year-old Palomo.

"Palomo," she says, "changed my life. I felt I had to return to teaching because he had so much to offer. If you give a pupil a fine horse, they become a fine rider.

"He is the most perfectly balanced horse I have ever ridden and he strives for perfection. But you ask him humbly, not tell him, and then he will show you how to do things properly.

"Palomo refuses to be a pedestal for someone else's ego and if they are too cocky or aggressive, he flips out. Riding him has to be a piece of music rather than a power struggle."

Sylvia has courteously hauled three people off the stallion, including a renowned international German trainer to whom the horse took great exception.

"Palomo went ballistic," she laughs, "and took a week to recover."

The equine also becomes angry if he sees Sylvia riding another horse, when he will furiously drum the stable floor with his front feet.

"This horse," says his doting owner, "turns sport into art and has given me the means of showing that to other people. He has also taught me that compassion and humility are among the requirements of a true horseman."

8 February 1996

The Kangaroo who is driving Karen crazy

National four-in-hand driving champion Karen Bassett recalls
her bumpy ride to the top with the talented and tireless
Kangaroo, who always insists on being top dog

K ANGAROO is a horse who thinks he is a dog, but cannot decide whether he is a Jack Russell or a Border Collie. He will be starring in a carriage driving road show next month, and will then point his owner towards the World Championships in Brussels later this year.

"Roo" is nearside leader for the top female international four-in-hand driver Karen Bassett, who is capable of spending a week curled up in an armchair recounting tales about her horse.

For, like a Jack Russell, Kangaroo can sham lameness, only in his case it is to avoid being ridden in the school. Years ago, a vet would be summoned, but then the penny dropped. If Roo was turned towards the gate as if to go hacking, he miraculously became as sound as a bell.

His Border Collie streak appears when Karen builds a twisty course of cones, turns the horse loose and directs him — as in the *One Man and His Dog* TV programme — by shouting "come" for right, "get" for left, "forwards" for straight on, and whistling for him to trot to her side.

No one could say horses were stupid after meeting Roo, a 16.3hh dark brown gelding. This clever and altogether nasty piece of work can head butt or pull Dan, the offside leader, by his breast collar in the direction he thinks they ought to be travelling. If Roo is in a foul mood, he will wait for a car to pass the carriage and then try to shoulder Dan into its path.

Surely these are fairy tales ...?

"No," says Karen. "Roo is a devil. I doubt whether there is a more intelligent horse in Britain. He is the leader of the team and it is his team. If I put a new horse next to him, he immediately shows it who is boss. First he shoves them with his hip and then, if they get in front of his nose, he bites them. If he gets really cross, he kicks them in the belly. To confirm his superiority, he tries to push them into traffic.

"Poor Dan took all the punishment and then retaliated. He and Roo had some terrible punch-ups and made each other lame several times. I had to let them sort it out for themselves, though."

By the time Karen met Roo, she was hardened to difficult equines. She began driving at eight years old because the Shetland pony she rode would throw and then trample her. Her mother sold the pony, only to have it returned a week later, so, in desperation, she broke it to harness.

Since then, Karen has won the National Championship seven times, twice with Shetlands, four times with her impossibly behaved spotted ponies and is currently National Champion with the Muschamp Trakehner team of horses.

This 32-year-old woman dominates a man's world and achieves it with her headache called Roo.

Fair haired and 5ft 9ins, Karen is based at Manor Farm, Henley-on-Thames, Oxfordshire, where, with business partner David Rooke, she runs a driving school which is shortly to expand into the weddings and funerals business.

But her success has not come easily — neither the horses nor trying to find the £35,000 necessary for a season's competing. This is why, in a bid to raise funds for her 1996 campaign, she is again launching the Carriage Driving Road Show, a seven-day touring show starting at Sands Farm, West Sussex on 4 March.

Roo will be doing what he likes best — performing in front of a crowd. He is the British National Champion's horse who really should not be in Britain at all. Twelve years ago, his dam, who was bought in Germany, was left at Walter Lorch's Muschamp Stud in Buckinghamshire, before being moved to Australia.

The owners paid for several months' livery and mysteriously disappeared, never to be seen again. The mare was called Aussie and, later, out hopped Kangaroo.

At two, he was a rig and nearly died under an anaesthetic. At three and four, he overturned Walter's carriage. Then Karen came on the scene and on Valentine's Day in 1991, the horse who can "bolt in walk" became a wheeler.

From the box seat, Kangaroo is the left leader

Karen was forced to swap him to nearside lead in the middle of an event and nervously held her breath, waiting for the explosion.

Roo, though, was happy in his own way, which meant for the next four years he was brave at hazards, tireless on marathons and made a mockery of dressage by hopping like one of his namesakes or doing extended trot throughout a test.

"I wanted to murder him," says Karen. "He thought it was all a big game, but now, thankfully, he has grown up a bit."

Today, in the sport which has the same dressage test throughout a season, Roo knows his stuff by heart and can still behave like a saint — almost.

However, he still relishes a fight and strives for a car accident involving Dan, but only between the months of January and March when he is brought back into training after the winter rest.

"He's an old ..." says Karen, using the impolite word for turf, "but he is utterly dependable. He helped me win the National Championships. Dan was having an off day, but once I had slowed down to let Roo push and pull through the first three hazards, Dan's confidence returned and we were flying again.

"Roo belongs to me now and I would never sell him. He is just a special horse. Hopefully, we will get a medal in the World Championships."

15 February 1996

The gangster who cruised alone

Team chaser George Goring recalls his 15-year partnership
with Bugsy Malone, who was fast, fearless and lived up to
his name

BUGSY MALONE used to be known as "Bugsy Alone" by team chasing aficionados because of the countless times horse and rider, in the shape of George Goring, parted company.

On one occasion, at the Berks and Bucks open, Bugsy said farewell to George at the 12th fence of 35, but Diana Clarke, who was leading the team and had not noticed him fall, carried on "talking" to George, as she could still see Bugsy out of the corner of her eye, jumping fluently and steering neatly through the flags.

"Watch out for this one, George," she shouted. "That's a bit close. George! Keep back."

Only when they finished did she realise that she had been addressing a riderless horse.

Bob Baskerville made the same mistake at the Atherstone.

"For God's sake, George, keep off my tail," he yelled at fence 29, when, in fact, George had left the team at fence three. That was the time George Goring of the Boring Gorings walked two miles to the finish to hear the commentator say: "Do not tell George, but the horse goes better without him."

And so Bugsy Malone became the first horse in team chasing to be awarded his own bottle of champagne.

George Goring says he needs good horses because he is such a bad rider, and he thinks

Bugsy was brilliant. Owner of the elegant Goring Hotel in London's Victoria, George has been Hotelier of the Year — but never rider of the year.

He took part in 104 point-to-points, but never won a single one, was an enthusiastic show jumper who fell off frequently at the first fence and an avid hunter trialler who was beaten by his 10-year-old daughter.

When Douglas Bunn, Master of Hickstead and Master of the Mid-Surrey Farmers' Draghounds, created the first team chase in 1974, he invited George to join his team on the proviso that he bring Bugsy Malone. Douglas thought a lot of the horse and little of the rider.

Once, out hunting, he had seen a body lying prone in a ditch and as he rode by had enquired: "Who is that?" On being informed that it was George, he replied: "Oh, good."

The Master's feelings for the horse were entirely different. He admired and respected Bugsy Malone.

The Mid-Surrey Farmers' Drag team came fifth at that first team chase and George, who managed to finish at the same time as Bugsy, was smitten by this new sport.

Bugsy, who did not know the word "refuse", was ideal transport. The 16.2hh liver chestnut gelding by a Thoroughbred out of a $\frac{3}{4}$ Thoroughbred mare, came over from Ireland after hunting there. George saw the horse looking weary in a Surrey stable with a price tag of £1,000 and reluctantly agreed to try him. He was delighted to find that, over fences, the horse operated on the automatic ballistics principle — the rider merely had to point in the right direction while the horse aimed and fired.

George took Bugsy home to Wrotham in Kent, where he was kept away from the manege, because George does not believe in schooling, and even further away from his wife Jenny's dressage horses, in case they spoke to Bugsy.

"Dressage horses are only good for dressage," he says.

Their first outing was with the draghunt where George being George and Bugsy being a bit of a gangster, they ignored advice to stay at the back and take it quietly. Instead, they went down what is known as the "Aintree line" ahead of the field — and in ripping style.

"I could have stopped him," says George, "but he was jumping fantastically and enjoying himself so much that I did not want to spoil the fun."

George Goring reckons that there is no greater trait in horses than enthusiasm.

"Bugsy," he declares, "is the most enthusiastic horse I have ever ridden."

George formed the Boring Gorings and today, at 57, holds a number of unofficial records. He is the only rider at the inception of the sport still competing. He also boasts that he only does open classes and reckons he falls more than anyone.

Bugsy conveyed him for 15 years in 100 team chases and the Boring Gorings' tally to date is around 20 wins, as many seconds, and a multitude of thirds.

The high spot of their partnership was in Czechoslovakia for the legendary Pardubice, a $4\frac{1}{2}$ mile race which includes the awesome Taxis fence, standing, according to George, 6ft 6ins with a 17ft-wide ditch on the other side, followed 200 yards later by a formidable Irish bank.

"You have to go like stuff of a shovel," says George poetically, "and Bugsy cleared the Taxis by three feet and steadied himself for the bank. I closed my eyes, kicked and left it to him. At 13, he knew what he was doing. He was fantastic and did not make a mistake. We were in front until the third from last when we were overtaken and came seventh."

When Bugsy Malone retired from work four years ago, fewer fiddles were as fit, but George says: "I loved him and he would have gone on until he dropped. He never dreamed of saying no, so I said no for him."

At 27, Bugsy looks like a Yeti, and still bosses the younger horses, but he calms the fractious when they first go into the field and only incites them to riot when George wants to bring them in.

"He was, and still is, the epitome of excellence," George says. "I defy anyone to say they have received more from a horse than George Goring received from Bugsy Malone."

When the old horse is laid to rest, George can take comfort from the videos of their past glories, although most will feature Bugsy Malone wearing his saddle, with reins and stirrups flapping, as he flawlessly cruises an accurate course alone.

22 February 1996

The cob with attitude

Journalist and amateur show rider Muriel Bowen recalls her
successful partnership with Cromwell, the prima donna showman
who produced nine Hickstead and three Royal Show wins

CROMWELL had expensive tastes. One bite of a violet cream from Fortnum and Mason — as a special thank you for winning at the Royal Show — and he spat out his regular Mars bar.

He was also a big time cob who only bothered to move when he could perform to a huge crowd with a rousing band and where there was plenty of room to gallop.

By the time journalist Muriel Bowen partnered him, Cromwell had been there, done it, bought a Horse of the Year souvenir and was "resting" like an actor.

Wondering why she had not seen the Irish-bred horse on the circuit for some time, Muriel wrote to his owners to find out if he was well and whether she could lease him. The net result was that she had him on hire for three months for £300, had only sat on him a couple of times, but found him suitably quiet and lazy, so duly entered his name as a late entry for Hickstead.

Nine-year-old Cromwell was a former Cob of the Year with four Hickstead championships under his belt. If he had been a wartime Spitfire he would have painted several "kills" on his white fuselage, to indicate the judges he had run away with and the grooms he had unseated because they had thought, unwisely, that he ought to "work in" like normal horses.

At 52, Muriel was an amateur, a riding club member who mounted a horse from an upturned bucket and described the manoeuvre to be as difficult as "trying to raise the dead".

She had owned a show horse years before, but her main aim was to escape Fleet Street from time to time "by visiting nice shows, eating picnics and having a ride on a smart horse in between".

Any professional could have predicted what happened next at Hickstead. When Muriel asked the horse to work in, he hardly put a foot forward, and she did not like to push the matter. Cromwell's walk and trot were manageable, his canter was short-lived, while the gallop became a bolt.

"I did not do anything to stop him because I was incapable of it," admitted Muriel. "I sat praying that he would stop with the others. He did, briskly turned himself in towards the judge and strutted round at the walk at a rate of knots. It was all quite alarming."

In the following week's *Horse & Hound*, the show reporter wrote: "It was sad to see Cromwell going as a shadow of his former self."

If she had written instead: "It was good to see Cromwell back and well done to his new rider," Muriel Bowen would never have bothered to ride in a ring again.

However, as a feisty Irish woman, among the first few females in the front line of journalism, cool in hot zones and comfortably jousting words with Britain's leading politicians, the cutting, short sentence in *Horse & Hound* provoked the same reaction as forgetting to switch off a whistling kettle — she steamed, bubbled and made a lot of noise.

There was to be a new regime for Cromwell at his yard near Horsham, West Sussex, run by show horse producer Maggie Griffin: plenty of grass, no oats and a new port bit. For Muriel's part, as she was unable to ride regularly and wanted to be fit, she took up jogging along the River Thames besides her Chelsea flat.

By the time the Royal Windsor Show rolled around, Muriel was a woman with attitude.

articles to *Horse & Hound* and writing obituaries for *The Times*.

"Cromwell was magic. Every time we won something, I would think 'it was great while it lasted', but there was always more to come. I liked beating the professionals because they were horsemen and I was only an amateur rider. Cromwell liked the big occasion, when he would really lower and gallop."

Outside the ring, Muriel became the motivator for cob classes to be held for amateurs, raising £100,000 in sponsorship and serving a term as president of the British Show Hack, Cob and Riding Horse Association, much respected for her knowledge and enthusiasm.

Cromwell was now under her thumb and the pair beat a line of professionals, only to be faulted because the greenhorn rider forgot the lap of honour.

She bought Cromwell for £1,000 and had eight and a half seasons with him. They won nine championships at Hickstead and three at The Royal. They also scored a frustrating seven seconds at the Royal International, while the Wembley crown eluded them too. Muriel has lost count of the number of county show wins, but remembers clearly that their prize-money totalled £4,879 — one of the highest amounts in cob history.

Cromwell ran away twice more with judges, developed the quirk of wanting to dispense with the boring preliminary judging in Ring Five and heading straight for Hickstead's International Arena for his championship, and was best "worked in" by riding him when the coaches unloaded the WI ladies and OAPs, because, says Muriel, "he loved people and being fussed over".

Muriel is 70 now and, although long retired from the ring, is still a working journalist, contributing

Cromwell retired when he was 17 and continued to be a prima donna. Maggie Griffin gave up the struggle of keeping him in the confines of a field and allowed him to wander around her property. Twice he disappeared and must have gone out on the lanes, but knocked on the door punctually at 5pm for supper.

He was put down in August 1989, a year and a half after retiring, and Maggie held him for the vet. To hide her red eyes, Muriel wore dark glasses to the office for a week. Her colleagues, normally cynical about people, were genuinely sympathetic about her horse, offering words of comfort and invitations to have a drink.

"Cromwell was a true cob," says Muriel, "and not all those who win cob classes are cobs. He was a horse who was in total command of himself and believed that he was the greatest.

"My success with him was beyond my dreams — he so enriched my life. I have never had another horse, or indeed human, who gave me so many happy surprises."

29 February 1996

The rogue who set a Shining Example

Harvey Smith recalls how he tamed a brilliant but delinquent
horse who was a bit like himself — a professional with a mind
of his own

WITH his tie tucked in his shirt and hands in his pockets, Harvey Smith quietly stood away from the crowd. No emotion showed on his granite-carved face as he watched a show jumping jockey being taken for a ride by a brute of a horse.

The venue was Dublin and Harvey had often spied the enactment of this particular scene on the circuit. The horse was a dirty stopper, whose aim then was to spin and cart the jockey out of the ring at a speed more familiar on the race track.

In Harvey Smith's eyes, the horse was not to blame, and he could no longer bear to see the disintegration of a potentially brilliant athlete.

"They were not riding him right," he says in his blunt Yorkshire way, and seized the moment in 1981 when the nine-year-old gelding and disappointed owners were in the process of throwing in the towel. Harvey handed them £2,000 or £3,000 — he cannot remember which — but declares cheerfully that either sum was "cheap enough", and it was not merely for yet another bargain difficult horse to reschool and sell on.

This was Harvey harvesting a golden family horse on which he was to win the first £25,000 offered in his sport, leave Milton and Warren Point standing way behind him and, more importantly, entice his elder son Robert home again, as well as accompanying younger son Steven in the Olympic Games.

The Dutch-bred 17hh chestnut was known as "Norman", and ready to conquer anyone who dared to trespass in his stable. He was long-strid-ing, strong, sharp as a hot knife through butter, fast and immensely careful over his jumps. He was soon to bring true meaning to his registered name, Shining Example.

"He had become too clever and cunning, had started stopping and would not go into the ring," says Harvey, "but he had a head full of brains."

"Doctor" Smith's treatment was a regular dose of persistent and determined "accuracy", plus practical application of his belief that "horses, like children, have to know they have no chance of getting the upper hand".

Harvey Smith was always accurate at presenting a horse to a fence and explained how Norman was launched on the road to ruin.

"It is when you 'miss' and let them down that you get trouble, because the careful horses do not want to hurt themselves."

This charismatic, self-taught star who represented Britain in two Olympics, 70 winning Nations Cup teams and won every national championship, took the newly confident and reformed delinquent on the circuit and says: "You knew when you went into a class that you had a chance of winning. He used to win two classes every show, taking on the best in the world. He won everything, speed classes, Derbys, Grands Prix and World Cups, and that takes a very special horse."

Man and horse appeared alike. Both were strong, professional, with minds of their own and occasionally grumpy. But they clearly clicked because Harvey took the time to teach Norman the circus tricks of sitting and lying down.

Back in the 1980s, Harvey had a whole string of top-class jumpers and most needed a number two jockey. He held out Shining Example as the carrot. Robert, who was 22 at the time and working in another yard, remembers the call from his father.

"He wanted me to come back to work for him and he gave me the horse to ride. Mind you, he borrowed Shining Example back again whenever he wanted him."

His father chalked up, at a guess, £300,000 on the chestnut and Robert swept up corners he had missed, including the Grands Prix at the Royal International and Wembley.

The youngest Smith was next in Shining Example's saddle. Because his father and brother were both professionals, they were exempt from the Los Angeles Olympics, so Steven had the privilege of riding him and went on to win a team silver medal.

He speaks humbly about the horse: "I had ridden all my life, but never something of that quality. Shining Example was a big step up for me. He taught me a lot and made me a better rider."

At home on his farm near Bingley, 600ft up on the Yorkshire moors,

Harvey Smith remembers walking the Olympic course with Steven and proudly praises his son for his cool behaviour at the sport's ultimate goal. He comments that the team would have won a gold medal if they had been touched by a bit of luck.

At 57, he still has a few show jumpers around the yard, but focuses on racing since his wife, Sue, holds a public trainer's licence. She is fast approaching a century of winners.

The man who ignited show jumping with his inimitable personality is now content to describe himself as her "assistant", although it is more like an equal partnership.

When the frost relented recently, a string of their racehorses could be seen amid plumes of warm breath on cold air, accelerating along the gallops.

A horse on the other side of a stone wall ceased grazing, lifted up his head with pricked ears and watched them pass. Shining Example, who was cheeky in his stable and is cured of his once recalcitrant behaviour in front of the fences he feared, is enjoying retirement aged 24.

Ask the Smith men what they liked most about the horse, and all three, though miles apart, used exactly the same words. Robert in Hertfordshire said: "He was a winner." Steven in Norfolk echoed the sentiment.

Their father in Yorkshire used the identical phrase, but added as only the great Harvey Smith could: "I love the old 'oss. If I did not, he would be in meat tins."

14 March 1996

The "quality tank" who outflanked the communists

Chris Collins, the first British jockey to win the Pardubice since 1914, recalls his versatile Stephen's Society, the horse with all the qualities he admires in a human

THE undercover plot by the communists was probably one of the most bizarre and unsporting acts in the Cold War and, like any spy thriller, involved the British Embassy, a heroine and a James Bond-type hero whose horsepower was not an Aston Martin, but a superior Thoroughbred.

It was Czechoslovakia 1974 and the communists wanted to oust British rider Chris Collins and his mount Stephen's Society from the Pardubice, one of the most formidable races in the world.

The Russians, though, had not been diligent in keeping their secret and a careless word was picked up by the British Embassy and the heroine, a sympathetic Prague waitress.

They quietly warned the hero, who admits today: "There were several moves afoot to eliminate me from the race, but I worked out how to deal with them."

The antagonism had been provoked a year before when Chris Collins first entered the race with Stephen's Society.

In the communists' eyes, he was a decadent capitalist with no hope of success, and his horse, a seven-year-old, had yet to triumph on any track.

As a result, the Bulgars, Czechs, Russians and Germans thought the British entry of amusement and no serious threat.

But by the second last fence, their condescending smiles were wiped from their faces as Chris Collins and Stephen's Society galloped into the straight in the lead, cleared the last and held on to win by eight lengths.

The Union Jack was hoisted and our national anthem played, 6ft rosettes were presented, the horse was asked to print his hoof on a racecard and Chris, the first British jockey to win the Pardubice since 1914, donated his colours to the hippological museum.

The Russians were not going to allow a repeat performance when the victors returned the following year.

Learning of the plan, Chris Collins worked out that the attack would come before the Taxis and his prediction proved correct.

A Russian rode across him at the second fence and another jockey tried to push him off the track. It was a nasty skirmish which rattled Chris and his horse, but they retrieved their ground only for Chris to fall at the Taxis.

He remounted, caught up with the field and was unseated again at the third water fence. Undaunted, he got back in the saddle and triumphantly crossed the line in third place.

Of his first attempt in the Pardubice, Chris Collins comments: "It was one of the most special moments in my life."

Of his second attempt, he pronounces: "Unnerving".

Chris Collins, 56, had two successful careers running parallel, business and horses. In the former, he began by achieving the honours in accountancy examinations and then became involved in the repurchase of the family perfumery company, Goya. He helped restructure it, only to sell it again, this time to ICI.

Today, he has an office in London's Hyde Park with sporting prints on the wall and holds the title of vice-chairman number three in the £10 billion industrial company Hanson plc.

As a rider, he was leading amateur twice, won around 130 races point-to-pointing and under Rules and came third in the Grand National on Mr Jones.

His switch to horse trials was no less meritorious, for he achieved a team gold in the European Championships, World and European team silvers, plus the Tony Collings Memorial Trophy for the leading points scorer.

Stephen's Society, by Choral Society, was with Chris the longest of all his horses. He raced, was a brilliant hunter and became an advanced eventer whose dressage debut aroused the charitable comment: "It is a pleasure to see Stephen at an event."

He was found as an unraced four-year-old and Chris Collins says: "He was built like a quality tank, the beau ideal of a staying steeplechase type."

The dark brown 16.2hh gelding was a stayer who had the habit of getting his tongue over the bit and carrying his head to one side. He treated 4ft 6in steeplechase fences with a cavalier attitude, which Chris explains: "He was like a person with superior ability, who does not have to try. It entraps them into carelessness."

Stephen's Society was not even rated the best of the Collins string, but he was sweet natured and could steamroller his way through the roughest ground, which made him suitable for the Pardubice, as a third of it is under plough.

Chris also trusted him to concentrate his mind at a fence like the Taxis, 5ft high and 5ft wide, with a 16ft 6in ditch on the landing side.

In fact, when Chris first saw this obstacle, he thought he was the butt of a joke and being shown some sort of boundary.

He recalls how Stephen met the Taxis.

"He took off close to it, not throwing much of a leap and I thought we were going on our heads. In fact, he landed lightly and weaved his way through the odd faller."

Stephen's Society won five races, was pulled up in the Grand National, switched to eventing and then hunted with the Vale of Aylesbury. He was retired to Chris Collins's Buckinghamshire farm, a measure of his owner's respect.

One day, Chris arrived home and, not seeing Stephen around, asked his wife Susanne where the horse was?

"He has gone to heaven," she replied.

"I was very sad," said Chris Collins, "but so grateful to Susanne for having made such a difficult decision.

"Stephen was a great horse who had all the qualities I admire in people. He had courage, go and determination. I owed him an enormous debt, but how can you really thank a horse?"

21 March 1996

The equine confection who sometimes went sour

Show producer Allister Hood recalls that Brown Buzzard
treated his handlers like prey, but even those on the receiving
end remember him better for his elegance and style

THE front end of the horse was more akin to
the Great White Shark, hungry for flesh and
blood, while the rear end had the kick of a mule.

Once, a groom shimmied up the wall as fast as
Superman and dropped down into the adjoining
stable to escape his clutches.

Another lad was not so lucky and was taken to
casualty after Jaws clamped on to his shoulder,
picked him up and flung him as though he were
a bit of litter across the box, an incident which
occurred when the horse was in his dotage, and
had apparently "mellowed".

This was Brown Buzzard living beyond his
name, because he made any bird of prey seem
merely like a sparrow.

He was a stunning 15hh equine confection of
floating elegance, with "look at me" presence.

He started out as a show jumper, went on to be
a working hunter pony, was transformed into a
hack who won the Royal International and
Wembley in the same year, and changed careers
again to become a celebrated hunter for whom no
country was too difficult.

On the way, he was partially responsible for a
marriage, and the founding of a dynasty of show
riders, wholly responsible for the ruination of two
expensive wristwatches, and the centre of a difficult diplomatic manoeuvre.

It started when Anne Collins, groom to Tom

and Edna Hunnable of Towerlands, was looking for a working hunter pony for the
Hunnables' son Christopher. Anne was tipped
off about a neat little horse by Ardmoss with a
£2,000 price tag. Buzzard was in the rough
when Anne first saw him and recalls today: "I
thought he would make a lovely worker, but an
even better hack."

Christopher Hunnable finished three working
hunter pony classes and won all of them that
year, while Buzzard wrapped up a fourth when
he jumped Chris off at a double and completed
the course alone.

Anne, though, became more convinced that
Buzzard would not only make a better hack, but
the best hack, and somehow had to convince the
Hunnables that he should change roles and
become a horse they neither needed, nor wanted.

She already had the jockey in mind, Allister
Hood, winner at that time of three Wembley titles,
and the man she was courting in one of the best
kept secret romances on the show circuit.

Anne's delicate ploy was to tell the Hunnables
that as Chris was at boarding school and unable
to ride during term time, it would be sensible to
keep Buzzard ticking over and continue his education by allowing Allister to ride him at Suffolk
County.

"I remember Anne saying he was a fantastic little horse," says Allister, "but the first time I saw him he went for me with his teeth bared and I ran out of the stable. I thought he was dangerous."

Allister never entered the Buzzard's box again, leaving Anne to cope admirably with the man-hating horse's quirks.

However, the curious fact was that once he was outside his own territory and under saddle, he could have been a role model for a police horse training school.

"A baby could have sat on him safely," says Allister. "He was a saint, a perfect horse with the most amazing ride. He never needed hours of schooling or working in, he just reserved his best for the ring. He had charisma and charm, and the busier and noisier the show, the better and calmer he went."

Brown Buzzard was the first horse Anne and Allister produced together, helped to cement their partnership and through him, too, they became known as a couple on the circuit.

Anne got her wish and saw her future husband ride Buzzard to victory at Suffolk County and go on to take third place at the Royal International and finish second at Wembley.

In 1981, the following year, they stormed to victory at both the International and Horse of the Year Show, the last hack to achieve this double. Mrs Hunnable was in the audience at the Royal International and applauded so enthusi-astically that her watch broke, spilling out its diamonds onto her lap and the floor.

Buzzard was sold in 1982 to the Cooper family and, now ridden by Stella Harries, was Horse of the Year Show champion again, but came second in 1983, the year Anne and Allister married.

Among the first clients at their new showing yard, Buttons Farm in Norfolk, were the Coopers, bringing with them Brown Buzzard.

All of them felt that the little horse, who had won the majority of hack championships around Britain, had nothing more to prove in the ring. Instead, he was hunted with the Cottesmore by Joan Gibson, before switching to Badsworth country, partnering 25-year-old farmer John Coxon, who also lost a valuable watch because of Buzzard's behaviour.

John had four seasons with him and says: "He was a grand chap out hunting, but a devil in the stable. He put me in hospital after picking me up and throwing me across the box one day, but he never scored with his kicking, although it was not for want of trying.

"If I told him off he would put his head down between his front legs and clap his teeth together as if showing remorse, and then have another go two seconds later."

The gelding was put down two years ago and buried at John's home in Thorne, near Doncaster. There was a wooden cross marking the place in the paddock, but another horse, a crib-biter, chewed it to bits.

The Hoods, now with four children – three of whom have ridden at Wembley – had one of their many scrapbooks on the table in front of a glowing log fire in the drawing room.

They showed me a commentary on Brown Buzzard in *Horse & Hound*, which stated: "He performs with elegance and style not too often seen." The writer added: "He never flinched in the roar of Wembley. Artistry is fine, but temperament is everything".

Clearly the writer of that praise had never met Brown Buzzard in his stable.

28 March 1996

The matchmaker who found his perfect partner

Point-to-point champion Ian McKie recalls his winning partnership on the beautifully balanced Man Of Europe, whose timing was exquisite

IT was not his future wife who immediately caught Ian McKie's admiring glance across a crowded field, but her horse, which he says "was the most impressive I had ever seen".

And, he adds with a small measure of gallantry and a large chuckle, "she did not look bad either".

In fact, having spotted Man Of Europe, he would not have cared had the Thames been on fire. The brown gelding's talents had already been merited by trainer Bertie Hill to be of "Olympic potential" providing the horse could rid himself of an annoying quirk.

While Man Of Europe had completed Chatsworth horse trials with a clear round, he had picked up an incredible 96 time-faults – all because he had planted his feet and refused steadfastly to move again, even though he was nowhere near a fence.

His owner, who was to become Mrs Victoria "Tocky" McKie, thought this handsome horse could be cured of his eccentricity by doing some

team chasing, which was where Ian McKie came in.

"I thought I had better investigate this fantastic horse a bit closer, so I bought the 'girl' a hot dog, and she suggested that as I liked the horse so much, I ought to come over to ride him."

This informal invitation was to lead to so much. "Jerry", as Man Of Europe was known at home, contributed towards Ian becoming point-to-point champion and Joint-Master of the Bicester, following in his father-in-law's footsteps.

Ian McKie knew a good horse when he saw one. Starting with the Pony Club, he had shown ponies at Wembley before graduating to small hunters. He was then talent-spotted by David Tatlow, the race-rider and show exhibitor, who suggested Ian spent his school holidays at his yard. The young jockey's parents were not amused when he threw over an Army career to continue full-time riding with David, hunting, showing and race-riding.

Ian considered Jerry among the most exciting of horses. "He was pure class," he says reverently. "He just floated, was beautifully balanced and accurate over an obstacle. Jerry was exceptional."

Tocky Sumner and Ian McKie took turns hunting with Jerry before deciding to point-to-point him. Tocky won a maiden on him, but, after a few more races, was mortified to read advice for punters about Man Of Europe, which stated starkly: "To be left alone when owner-ridden."

Tocky's prized horse by Harwell out of Gainstown Lass was literally being prized away from her, but only with her blessing.

Ian and Jerry's partnership produced 15 wins, including four under Rules.

"The most thrilling evening of my life was at Cheltenham when we beat two *Horse & Hound* Cup winners," says Ian. "We came to the last fence a couple of lengths behind, jumped it and landed a length clear, passing the leaders in the air. I'll always remember the roar of the crowd and Tocky crying with happiness."

Ian jokes that he had to propose to the daughter of John Sumner, who bred and owns Dublin Flyer, in order to keep the ride on the 17hh gelding. The couple married in 1979 and celebrated Ian's championship, fuelled by six wins on Jerry, a year later.

Among their successes was the Coronation Cup

at Larkhill where they picked off the contenders one by one until it was Man Of Europe and Dance Again vying over the last fence. Ian, 38, recalls: "He negotiated obstacles with precision and a minimum of effort, conserving his energy to produce a turn of speed which was electric, but it was all to do with timing.

"Once at Warwick I was too impatient and cocky and was beaten because I hit the front too early. The horse's head came up as if to say, 'That's it, I have done enough'. You could not force an issue with him – he could make you look a complete buffoon or absolutely brilliant."

A virus struck Man Of Europe shortly after Ian McKie's second championship title and he and Tocky decided that their much loved horse would rest and return to less arduous team chasing and hunting.

The couple, who have two children, had by now bought Twyford Mill, Capt Ian Farquhar's former Buckingham home, where they farm 600 acres and 39-year-old Tocky has a licence to train.

There are 22 stables around the house and the horse who used to bang most and loudest on the door of his box for peppermints and attention was Jerry. Although he never lost his penchant for digging in his toes and refusing to budge while working alone, Ian says: "He was the finest you could ever wish to ride behind hounds."

In 1985, when hounds were on the Bicester/Marylebone railway line with a train imminent, Ian and Man Of Europe jumped the wire on the embankment, picked up the hounds, skipped over the line, popped up the opposite bank and went out over the wire.

A few months later, a girl groom was hacking him out in the snow, when 15-year-old Man Of Europe's knee was broken by a kick from another horse. The McKies were in tears when the vet put him down.

"It was like losing one of the family," says Ian.

"We were devastated," says Tocky.

Ian has the final word. "He was an intelligent horse who had developed his own ideas but he taught me how to ride, how a high-class horse feels, and how to be patient and sympathetic. He tested my bravery and skill. More than that, everything I have now is because of Man Of Europe."

4 April 1996

The "world-class" hunter who jumped into the limelight

Derek Ricketts recalls his dazzling career with Hydrophane Coldstream, whose verve, courage and accuracy contributed to two team gold medals

THE wily Irish horse dealer must have kissed the Blarney Stone before approaching Derek Ricketts in the collecting ring after the show jumper's victorious Volvo World Cup qualifier on Hydrophane Coldstream in Dublin.

"To be sure," said the Irishman, "'tis a fine horse you have there, sir. I have his half-brother at home. You had best come and see him."

Derek Ricketts replied politely: "I don't think so, because that man approaching us bred and owns the horse."

The man walking towards them with a broad smile was Rodney Ward, founder and director of Hydrophane and a Joint-Master of the Grafton Hunt, who had put his father's 16-year-old mare to the HIS stallion Pollards.

Her only foal, Coldstream, was a 16.3hh bay with a high wither, who followed his dam into the hunting field when he was four. Rodney Ward was in no doubt that he was riding a horse of unlimited potential.

"He had a helluva jump," he proclaims. "I remember taking a large gate and only one other chap came over with me, so we had hounds to ourselves for about 20 minutes. The horse was absolutely brilliant."

The following year, Rodney's wife Glenda conferred with horse trials trainer Bertie Hill. Both decided that Coldstream was wasted hunting and

that he should go eventing. He won three novice events, a novice championship and an intermediate class. But as an eight-year-old, having gone clear at Badminton, he suddenly needed an operation for a split tendon.

Meanwhile, Derek Ricketts, a farmer's son who had sprung into the limelight at the age of 18 when he won the Foxhunter final, was feeling as gloomy as the Wards over the vagaries of keeping horses.

At the Royal International, Derek and top ride Beau Supreme had fallen in the King's Cup. Derek was thrown clear, but the horse broke a leg and had to be put down.

Derek was cheered up by a letter from Rodney Ward asking if he would be interested in taking on a three-day eventer. Derek rang Bertie Hill and then the owner. The horse, who was to consider his stable his castle and repel all marauders, was with Derek the next morning on his 60-acre farm in Bicester.

"Coldstream looked a quality horse and from the moment I started to jump him, I knew he was outstanding," he says. "He may not have looked the best, but he felt so good. He was careful and had tremendous power."

Derek Ricketts and Hydrophane Coldstream were about to become household names and reach the zenith of their careers together.

Their partnership began in 1976 when Coldstream was nine. They were at Wembley that

year and catapulted into the European Championships the following year in Vienna, where they were team silver medallists.

The next two years were equally dazzling, with team gold medals at the 1978 World Championships and the 1979 European Championships. As team members, Derek recalls that they never had more than four faults, but Derbys were their favourite competitions, where Coldstream's cross-country experience gave him nerve and courage.

They were successful from Wales to Dublin and on the continent – everywhere, in fact, but Hickstead, where they had a frustrating run of second place six times, with a different fence catching them on each occasion.

Derek says: "He never refused, flapped or even gave his fences a lot of room, but he was accurate. I could walk a course and never have to think, 'That's the bogey fence'. He could have won as much as Milton in Milton's day, instead he picked up sums of £1,025 for a World Cup qualifier plus two other classes. He was a horse before his time."

In 1984, when he was 17, Coldstream was retired after wining, at a guess, five cars and £100,000. He left the sport, which had only been a second choice, the way he entered it, on a high – winning a speed class at Wembley.

Coldstream returned home to Rodney Ward in Blakesley, Northamptonshire, and 10 days later was hunting with the Grafton.

His kidneys began to fail when he was 23 and Rodney telephoned Derek, inviting him to see the great horse for the last time.

"Coldstream was in a small field behind the stables and came trotting over to Derek," said his owner. "I am sure the horse knew what was going on and that he was glad Derek had come to see him on his final day."

Now 47, Derek is Field Master with the Bicester with Whaddon Chase. He is rarely seen in the ring, though, leaving his 17-year-old daughter Clare to carry on the family name.

A bronze of Coldstream, given to his owner by the Grafton subscribers and farmers, sits on a shelf in Rodney Ward's sitting room.

Derek Rickett's memories are contained in a bumper collection of photographs. He thinks Coldstream's epitaph should be short and sweet.

"World class," he says simply.

11 April 1996

The surly stallion who sired a string of winners

Breeder Robin Knipe recalls the glittering stud career of Celtic Cone, a tough and tireless stallion with a shocking temper, whose progeny were the victors of 452 races

ROBIN KNIPE was in Stoke Mandeville hospital with a broken back when nurses wheeled him in front of a television set to watch Royal Ascot – and what he saw changed his life.

It was a little horse with limitless stamina, and a preference for soft going, winning the Queen Alexandra Stakes with Willie Carson on his back on rock-hard going. "What a tough horse," thought Robin.

Back on his feet, and two years later, this former amateur race-rider sold his herd of 60 dairy cows to pay for Celtic Cone, the horse he saw on television. Those who knew Robin well thought he was taking a huge risk.

The horse was considered to be an unimpressive mover, lacking in bone and endowed with an extremely bad temper. The only two people who believed Robin's £10,000 gamble would pay off were his mother-in-law, the trainer Mercy Rimell, and John Magnier of the Coolmore Stud.

Robin's wife Scarlett, a show rider, winner of the Newmarket Town Plate and former champion point-to-point rider, merely reserved judgement until Celtic Cone came to cover his first grey mare. Then, she quickly came down on the side of those who had judged her husband insane and also decided that the horse was equally touched in the head.

It was dramatically apparent that Celtic Cone had a vicious prejudice against all grey mares. When one was offered to him, the stallion would bite huge chunks out her flesh and refuse to serve her, even though he would quietly do his duty with a mare of any other hue.

Robin eventually overcame this mystifying problem by using Celtic Cone's own green New Zealand rug on grey mares, which sufficiently confused the horse into performing like a gentleman.

There were times when Robin thought his change of career from dairy farming to breeding jump horses might have been a mistake, but they did not last long. One of Celtic Cone's first crop was Celtic Ryde, a top hurdler who put Cobhall Court Stud, set in 110 acres and four miles from Hereford, firmly on the map.

Celtic Cone arrived 1974 when he was seven and from 1988 to 1992 the celebrated 15.3hh liver chesnut with a chunky white whorl on his forehead was either the leading British-based National Hunt stallion, or the leading British-based sire of individual chase winners.

Celtic Cone sired the victors of 452 races worth more than £2 million, the best of whom included Celtic Shot, Celtic Ryde, Celtic Isle, Celtic Chief, Earth Summit, Ryde Again and Royal Cedar.

"In the beginning people would say, 'What did you buy that old devil for?' but I believed in him

miles, with an electric ability to change up a gear.

Celtic Cone was considered game and genuine, but possessed a shocking temper. He would take his bad moods out on the stable walls and paddock railings. He kicked so hard and so often that it was difficult to keep his hind shoes on, so the Knipes padded his box with rubber. At least four times a year Celtic Cone would work himself up so much that he gave himself colic.

At the height of his stud career he was serving 90 mares a season and was popular with owners of large mares, who wanted smaller progeny.

"As Celtic Cone was small," says Robin, "we had to drop the mares into a hollow, so he could stand over them. His undoubted early gift to us was that he was able to produce good horse from average mares."

Celtic Cone's unmitigated success at stud helped the Knipes buy decent mares and breed classy horses including Master Oats, the Tote Cheltenham Gold Cup winner, and Anzum who was unbeaten in seven consecutive races.

In fact, when the Thoroughbred Breeders' Association awards were presented recently, the racing press joked that the Monopolies and Mergers Commission ought to investigate the Knipes because Cobhall Court Stud swept the board.

Celtic Cone was the foundation of Robin's glittering career away from dairy farming.

"If he had not been so special, I would have been back milking cows," says Robin.

The horse's gravestone is marked simply "Celtic Cone, 1967 to 1992" and the fir trees growing on the grave at Cobhall annually drop a crop of cones.

Robin Knipe thought the decision to put him down was the hardest he had ever had to make in his life.

"I could not bring myself to do it, and I put it off for six months. He was arthritic and his coat was dropping out in handfuls, but I did not like to admit to myself that he was finished.

"I was seriously sad," he says, "and I was right about him being tough. The vet had to give him a double dose of injections to put him to sleep because he was so strong. He said that Celtic Cone had a real athlete's heart."

18 April 1996

because of his toughness," says Robin. "When he was in training for the Yorkshire Cup, the story goes that he needed one last good blow out so other horses were brought out to work with him. When Celtic Cone exhausted the first, the next one took over and, when that began to fade, the third one jumped in. When Celtic Cone was eventually pulled up, he kicked that horse.

"At Chepstow, Celtic Cone was in the championship for five-year-olds over hurdles when he fell at the last with the jockey miraculously remaining in the saddle. He got up and still won. The horse was just bloody-minded."

This stallion by Celtic Ash out of Fircone, who had 14 wins on the Flat and over hurdles, surprised his owner by the sort of horse he was producing. Celtic Cone showed his best form over long distances, but his progeny preferred 2, or $2\frac{1}{2}$

The hunter who soared like an angel on wings

Joint-Master of the Kildare, Charlie O'Neill, recalls the action-packed career of Abbeylands, who feared nothing, was a great galloper and earned honours as escort to the Irish President at the Royal Dublin Show

CHARLIE O'NEILL, Joint-Master of the Kildare and a director of Punchestown racecourse, firmly believes that God created Ireland for horses and that one of those gallant creatures should be canonised, or at least immortalised.

Charlie's chesnut gelding, Abbeylands, was considered to be an angel on wings, who flew over the sort of country which would turn the average rider's complexion white.

Even a Master from England had heard of the legendary Abbeylands and, when he turned up for a day with the Kildare, he stood in Charlie's yard eagerly asking the Irishman: "Which one is he?"

"That is Abbeylands," replied Charlie proudly.

Charlie O'Neill, a latter-day Flurry Knox with a lyrical way of speaking, never bothered to bolt the bottom of his hunter's door and, if he and his staff were exercising horses around their cross-country track, "Abbey" would let himself out and follow them over the fences.

"He was the finest horse I ever threw a leg over," declares Charlie.

He rode Abbey in the famous $4\frac{1}{2}$-mile Punchestown banks race, in which there is a formidable double.

"It is the biggest thrill that is ever put up in front of you," says Charlie with appreciation.

"The Pardubice is just 'trotting up' after it.

"Have you heard the poem: 'When you charge this affair, you can feel every hair/Stand on edge, as stiff as newly-cut stubble/And your heart misses a beat/When your horse changes feet, on the dome of the Punchestown double'. That sums it up exactly.

"They hollered me on to the bank and I hollered back. Abbey ate it up. He was foot perfect."

Abbey came 10th out of 18 runners that day, a creditable performance, considering all the others were Thoroughbreds, and his dam was a hairy-legged working horse, heavier built than an Irish Draught, and only inches shorter than a Shire.

Charlie recalls how, out hunting, they cleared a hedge and a reclamation ditch like a canyon.

"I was lodged in mid-air and the next thing I saw was a 3ft high electric fence. I said to myself: 'Bejayzus, we are going to have some fall here!' But we never touched a thing and people went back the next day to look at the size of the leap."

Abbeylands's career was action-packed — this 16.2hh gelding, at one time or another, carried a member of the Rolling Stones, all five of the O'Neill children and a visiting American who was so smitten he is buying a house in Ireland.

Abbey also represented Ireland in the team chasing finals at Cirencester, where Richard

Pitman, who was commentating, approached Charlie afterwards to compliment him on his horse.

Horse and rider won a point-to-point, hunter trials and cross-country races and paraded hounds at the Royal Dublin Show. There, Abbey caused a stir when he was acting as escort to the Irish President, who was being conveyed in a landau.

"It looked as if the horse was wired to the moon," laughs Charlie. "He was so berserk with excitement I thought we would land slap in the middle of the Irish band.

"To ride on that hallowed ground, on the horse I loved with all my heart, was my greatest moment — my greatest memory."

Charlie, a 54-year-old farmer, and his wife, Mary, live on the 250-acre establishment which gave the Abbeylands name to the horse. Twenty miles from Dublin, it has an equestrian centre, hireling business and cross-country course with a fence the O'Neills call "Bechers", where Abbeylands is buried.

Charlie bought the horse, by the Thoroughbred Dreamy Eyes, in 1970 as a yearling for £70 with £5 change for luck money. The pair was carried home in an open-topped cattle trailer, with Charlie hanging on to the youngster's head because he feared he might sail over the side.

As a four-year-old Abbey numbed Charlie's fingers and lit up his life as he pulled like a train across Ward Union country, often slipping the field and going away with hounds and stag.

Those were the days that were so often repeated later in Kildare country, when Charlie says the horse made him feel like a king, not merely trotting home after a day's hunting, but floating home.

"Abbey broke people's hearts as they tried to catch up with him across

country. He was a great galloper, had 10 legs, feared nothing and only stopped for a reason. I chastised him only once for stopping and then saw we would have landed on a harrow. I never queried him after that.

"People said we did crazy things, but they were never crazy because Abbey was outstanding. In his later years, I would go out and feed him at night and say to myself, 'What in the name of God will I do if I have to put him down? It will kill me as well as the horse'."

Abbeylands was to save his owner from what he dreaded most, because last year, during the final draw of the day, the 25-year-old horse had a heart attack and was dead before he hit the ground.

Charlie had left Abbey to be hunted lightly by a girl, while he led the field on a coloured horse. Word was sent forward to him and when he came back to his old horse, he found him lying with a hunting jacket draped over his shoulders with two women crying.

"They were in a terrible state," recalls Charlie. "The scene would have drawn a tear from a stone, but I was quite happy, because Abbey did not suffer."

25 April 1996

The oversized pony who had them all in a spin

Sent home from a Hunt, aggressive by nature and an escapologist to boot, who would have thought that Spinning Rhombus would evolve into a world-class eventer?

THE pint-sized Thoroughbred was the Sherpa Tensing of the equine world, prepared to take on Everest and consider it a molehill.

The final straw for his patient owners was when he was sent home from Bicester for climbing on the backs of other horses.

He was immediately dispatched to the equine reform school run by the Olympic New Zealand rider Andrew Nicholson, who thought him an oversized thug of a pony and nicknamed him Piggy because he squealed when he bucked.

But the delinquent was determined to escape the strict new regime. He climbed out of a field, out of his stable and made an attempt to squeeze through the 2ft gap at the top of the tail-gates of the lorry while it was parked at a riding club dressage competition.

Andrew, who was working in another horse, heard the commotion, saw a crowd of anxious people in the distance and found Piggy with his head and leg dangling over the front of the gates with his wither crushed against the roof, his headcollar broken and a partition smashed.

"It took some tugging to extricate him," says Andrew, "and once he was out, I thought I had better get on and ride him. He behaved like a gentleman and won the dressage."

Andrew's assessment was that the horse's mountaineering exploits were due to boredom and he telephoned his owner, Rosemary Barlow, to say he would keep Piggy for about six weeks, take him novice eventing and then send him home for her daughter Camilla to compete in Pony Club events.

Instead, Spinning Rhombus stayed five years and, under the New Zealand flag, won a team gold in the 1990 World Championships and a team silver in the 1992 Barcelona Olympics.

Andrew, a six-footer with a wicked wit, still finds it hard to believe their success. He considered the horse too small at 15.3hh, with minuscule talent, a know-it-all attitude and too aggressive in the show jumping ring.

Once when they were jumping an intermediate cross-country course, Piggy closed his ears and worked his trotters too fast, provoking Andrew into reminding him who was in charge. Piggy retaliated and ran straight into a corner, turning turtle in the process. After the rider had crawled out from underneath him, he decided in future the horse could cruise at what speed he found most comfortable.

"It was a painful lesson, but I learned not to aggravate him," Andrew said.

He added: "When I think of all the horses you look at as potential purchases, hoping they might be that 'super one', I can honestly say Piggy would not even have merited a second glance."

In fact, Andrew Nicholson always estimated the horse's limit was novice, "but he just gradually kept on doing enough to get to the other side".

The Kiwi's cool attitude and talent nurtured in racing stables were the perfect foil for the wayward gelding. The rider had considered school at Te Awamutu a place to pop in for a spot of lunch, meet the girls and play a bit of sport, nothing too excessive to interfere with the equestrian business. At 16, he was working for two trainers and would have sat on 20 young Thoroughbreds by lunchtime, when he would bicycle the 15 miles home to remake slow racehorses into show jumpers and eventers to sell on.

At 17, he was in Cirencester, England, working in a National Hunt yard and, on his days off, either competing on his own horse, or grooming for his former Kiwi neighbour Mark Todd, whose win at Badminton on Southern Comfort inspired him to follow the horse trials route.

At 28, with one Olympic Games behind him and now married to Jayne, Andrew put down roots at Pleasant Spot Farm, near Somerset, only to find the peace disturbed by the revolving Spinning Rhombus.

Finding that hard work civilised the horse, Andrew whisked him away, without any cross-country schooling, to three novice events in 10 days and they came second in each. Despite winning the fourth, Andrew still could not rate him highly.

"If he did not jump a fence, he climbed over it. I knew he was honest and enjoyed what he was doing, but I never dreamed the fat, hairy pony could ever go clear cross-country in the Olympics."

He only began to believe in the little horse years later, when they won Punchestown and a ticket to the World Championships.

Show jumping was Piggy's weak spot, but he had a familiar pattern of operating across country.

Andrew explained: "For the first minutes he was lethargic, next you felt him get rid of any virus you feared he might be suffering from, and then he would start flying when most other horses would be dropping their bits.

"As you neared the end of the course it would not have mattered what had been built because he would have had a go at it. His adrenalin over-ran his brain."

Spinning Rhombus was retired last year at the age of 14, having chalked up as many international three-day events as his number of years. He moved on to a new career, splitting the longest partnership Andrew Nicholson has shared with any horse.

"It felt like one of the family had left home to go to another job," he said.

Andrew is competing at Badminton and at the time of writing has three horses entered, so is in the unenviable position of being drawn first and last. He is also on the New Zealand short-list for the Atlanta Olympics.

And Piggy? He is a Master's horse at the Bicester – the Hunt that expelled him from the field nine years ago – and is bold, brave and impeccably behaved.

2 May 1996

The "novice" who could raise the Union Jack

Dressage trainer and European silver medallist Richard Davison rides his dream horse, Askari, in front of the Olympic selectors

IF Richard and Gillian Davison had been on one of those daft TV game shows for married couples, they would have waltzed away with the first prize.

Independently, on different days, they used exactly the same words to describe a raw, unfurnished potential Grand Prix horse and Richard Davison, dressage trainer and European silver medallist, says it was the only time the couple had agreed over anything.

It was that the horse had an unprepossessing trot, a gymnastic canter and was, basically, naturally talented. It was the horse Richard had waited 21 years for and will ride on Sunday (12 May) in front of the selectors for a nail-biting second time, when they select their short list to decide who goes to the Olympic Games.

Richard cannot believe his luck. Compared with this bay beauty with a sculptured head, some of his other rides can be likened to a pile of cowpats. That includes all those he bought as a teenager at the sales who reared, bucked or bolted, to a number of his Advanced horses who, down the years, would have tried the patience of St Francis.

Two of them spooked and blew up at Britain's crucial dressage venues, one at Stoneleigh over plastic jumping blocks used to dress the arena and the other over flapping flags and canvas at Goodwood.

Despite hanging a plastic block in the stable of the former and piling plastic sheets, canvas and bunting around the box of the other until it resembled a New Age traveller's encampment, it made no difference to their erratic behaviour.

The most exasperating of all was a horse with all the talent and a respiratory problem.

"Try making a perfect transition from passage to piaffe with a horse that wants to snatch the reins from you and pull you round its ears, while it stretches its neck to cough," exclaims Richard.

Today he cannot speak highly enough of Askari, the Dutch gelding with the Swahili name meaning "guard". It is not that he believes him to be one of the few naturally-talented Grand Prix horses in the world that excites him, nor that Askari can now trot on springs, dance through tests and obtain marks of eight and nine for the key elements. It is all the tiny bonuses that come with Askari's superlative temperament. Richard feels he can at last concentrate solely on dressage without any "ifs" or "buts".

Askari travels without fuss, lies down and relaxes at an international competition, where the stables can be busy with show jumpers clattering around until late in the night, does not mind flags, plastic or applause, and would lick his feed bowl clean or stand, if required, like a sentry in the middle of a full voltage Jean-Michel Jarre laser concert. He is also the most gentle and friendly horse at the Davisons' home at Combridge Farm in Staffordshire and adored by the two Davison children.

Equally important at this time in the equestrian calendar is that Askari, rising nine and lightly built, is young enough and the stamp of horse believed to be best able to cope with the humidity at Atlanta.

Richard, 40, usually the most prosaic of people, declares with gusto: "The horse is wonderful. If he was human he would be the sort of chap every mother would want their daughter to marry."

He found Askari, by Avignon out of a mare by the English Thoroughbred Darling Boy, in a Dutch yard when the gelding was four.

His wife Gill, a former point-to-point and horse trials rider, stepped in to do all Askari's basic training. Then the couple agreed that such a special equine, who found the difficulties of piaffe, passage and canter pirouettes easy, must have special treatment.

They decided it was pointless flogging Askari all the way through the grades and, instead, spent the time investing in some training.

Last year, Richard produced the horse, like a conjuror triumphantly pulling a rabbit out of a hat, and came fourth in their premier Grand Prix competition, third in the Grand Prix special at their first international outing, second in the National Championships, second in another international and fourth in a World Cup qualifier.

Askari won the award for the most exciting new Grand Prix horse and Good Friday this year turned into an excellent Friday when Richard and his dream horse won the first Olympic trial.

The delighted rider's only regret was that his father Gordon wasn't alive to see it.

He had ushered a protesting Richard into the family firm and even gave him his own petrol station in the hope it might fuel his interest in business.

Gordon gave up the battle after finding his son around the pumps late one afternoon, dressed in mud splattered hunting kit.

Today Richard Davison is a leading trainer and Fellow of the British Horse Society and is an inordinately proud possessor of a horse who has been billed as "a rising star" and "hot prospect".

Richard says: "There is more work to do on the finer points, but if I live to 100 I am not going to find a better horse, nor an easier one. Nothing concerns Askari, he just pricks his ears and goes."

He hopes the horse will fulfil all his praise in front of the selectors again on Sunday and reckons the hardest part will be waiting for the telephone call to say whether they have a ticket to Atlanta.

But it is no life or death matter for they have another six or seven years of international challenges ahead of them and at least one more chance of riding under the flag in the ultimate competition.

It is an attractive thought to harbour that Richard and Askari, who is still deemed a novice under British rules, could raise the Union Jack in America during 1996.

9 May 1996

The veteran athlete who behaves like a mule

Former champion jump jockey Peter Scudamore recalls the successful racing career of Sabin Du Loir whose honesty, guts and zest took him to the winner's enclosure 23 times

ELEVEN-YEAR-OLD Thomas could not have been more proud or confident about a successful outcome, as he set off with his celebrated father in a pairs class at a local hunter trial.

Just minutes later, and red with embarrassment, Thomas steered his pony off course in utter disdain, leaving a chaotic scene behind him. Lying cheerfully on the ground was his dad, Peter Scudamore, eight times champion jump jockey and the first ever to ride 200 winners in a season.

Lying next to him was Scu's horse, Sabin Du Loir who, in his heyday, beat Waterloo Boy and Desert Orchid, won more than £250,000 in prizemoney and whose courage over fences has been recognised by naming a race after him at Newbury.

Together, they had been victors of two hurdle races and 11 steeplechases, but at the Pony Club hunter trial the heroes were caught out by a mere 2ft 6ins tiger trap, which necessitated a gentle approach at trot, down a slight slope.

"It was only tiny," says Peter Scudamore, "but Sabin was not used to tackling things quite so slowly. We lay on the ground looking at each other thinking, 'Do we really need this at our time of life?'"

Sabin Du Loir ran only 38 races in his career, winning 23, including the Sun Alliance Hurdle at Cheltenham, in performances which were described as "zestful".

In his last year on the track, aged 13, this $2\frac{1}{2}$-miler won three in a row and, in his final challenge, the John Bull Chase at Wincanton, he beat Ryde Again in typical formidable, fighting style.

He led until headed, made a mistake three out, whacked the second last, and then, with only a tap down his shoulder, clawed back the lead in the last strides.

With that flourish he hung up his racing plates, left Martin Pipe's yard and his Guernsey owner, Brian Kilpatrick, and went home with Peter Scudamore, determined that retirement should mean resting and feasting.

Peter Scudamore MBE, aged 37, is also retired, having quit race-riding three years ago despite hundreds of his punter fans writing to beg him not to.

Scu had anticipated that Sabin would fit in well with his new life as a journalist, TV commentator and trainer in partnership with Nigel Twiston-Davies whose yard adjoins his land near Cheltenham.

Sabin would make an ideal trainer's hack — or so Scu had thought.

"Sabin will not go on the gallops," declares Scu.

"If you take him to the entrance he walks the other way saying 'I am retired. I do not do that sort of thing'.

"Sabin will condescend to school over fences, but not with me, he refuses with me. I do not know what it is. He jumps for my eldest son Thomas, a young lady, and a couple of lads in the yard, but not me. He is a monkey but seems to know who he has to look after."

The 17-year-old bay gelding never napped on the track, indeed his *modus operandum* was to carry Scu off a long stride, or a very, very long stride and rattle the tops of the fences, with Britain's former Number One jockey grabbing a handful of mane so that he would not interfere with Sabin's mouth.

Sabin Du Loir by Go Marching and with a French grandam, today refuses to show jump but eats up North Cotswold country behind hounds with either Scu or his wife Marilyn.

He also occasionally hacks out with three generations of the Scudamore family from their inappropriately named home, "Mucky Cottage".

There is grandpa Michael Scudamore, who won 500 races including the Grand National and Cheltenham Gold Cup, Scu and his two sons Thomas, now 13, and 11-year-old Michael.

What Scu had most wanted, though, was for Sabin to carry young Thomas to the start of the Sabin Du Loir race at Newbury.

But in a practice canter which entailed passing the entrance to the gallops, the horse napped and dropped the boy.

It is a measure of how strong Peter Scudamore's feelings are for Sabin when he nobly excuses the horse's behaviour.

"He's a powerful horse for a boy and Sabin was doing his best to look after him. Things can go wrong when you are on a horse," he says.

Peter, who will be saddling runners at Aintree tonight (16 May) and at Bangor on Dee on Saturday, admits he misses the thrill of race riding and the camaraderie of the weighing room, but not the hospitals, hard work and wasting.

All that is in the past, along with Sabin Du Loir, which is precisely what makes the horse so special to the former jockey.

"He is an old mate from the old days," says Peter. "On the racetrack Sabin had all the traits you admire, guts, honesty and fantastic athletic ability. There have been better horses with more charisma, but not such character."

He adds: "He eats a lot today. You could say eating is his favourite pastime."

16 May 1996

The "uncontrollable" chaser who always repaid his debts

Showman and former point-to-point jockey Vin Toulson recalls
National Hunt star, Panhandle, whose glittering career in the
1950s was curtailed by his mysterious death

WHEN Panhandle was taken to the Remount Depot for a loose school down the jumping lane, his owner, solicitor's daughter Daphne Marsh, was dismayed to see him hesitate over a tiny obstacle with a ditch on the take-off side.

Suddenly, Panhandle found his confidence, popped it, and ripped cleanly over the rest like a typhoon hitting Texas, not even stopping at the 6ft fence at the end. He soared over that, too, and was finally caught at Melton bus station.

Three days later, Panhandle and his intrepid lady jockey lined up at the Cottesmore point-to-point, politely allowing the other contenders to get halfway to the first fence before they set off, to avoid any interference. By the second fence the arm-wrenching Panhandle was in the lead, four from home, plus a fence clear of the other runners, when he unsurprisingly blew up and fell.

Panhandle was many things, but never a slug. He once dropped a groom, covered four miles at

Vin Toulson and Panhandle leap into the lead at a hunter chase at Nottingham

racing pace along a main road, trotted up sound the next morning and won at Nottingham that afternoon.

Daphne Marsh discovered the only way she could control him at a pace faster than a slow canter was to work him on the site of an old Roman encampment with a vertical hill, where he would agreeably apply the brakes at the top.

When she came to grief in an accident on another horse, she called up the main man in local point-to-pointing to deputise temporarily for her on Panhandle.

"It was disastrous," she says. "After one race and a schooling session, he said he did not want to ride him again and I asked if he could think of someone else. 'There is only one chap,' he suggested, 'who enjoys riding horses that are a challenge.'"

Whether through malice or generosity, Daphne was given the name of Vin Toulson, a point-to-point champion and son of a farmer, horse dealer and show ring rider.

The new combination crashed out, too, at their first attempt, but persevered for another few races between the flags until Vin Toulson, who had iron instead of blood in his veins, recognised that the horse could not go the distance, and was in fact a two-miler who should race under Rules.

Panhandle, the 50 guinea sky-gazing skeleton from Leicester Sales and described by Daphne and Vin as an "uncontrollable nutcase", became a National Hunt star of the 1950s. The number of occasions he came second have been lost in the mists of time, but he won six and was improving each time, when his glittering career ended abruptly with his mysterious death.

The bay Thoroughbred gelding brought exhilaration and reward to four people: a local pensioner who backed Panhandle and won sufficient to pay for his winter fuel and rent; the girl who led him in the paddock, whose bets reaped enough for her first mortgage deposit; Daphne Marsh, who became Mrs Toulson and her husband Vin, who used Panhandle's prize-money to help them buy Gartree Stud in Leicestershire, and to start dealing in quality horses.

Today, 65-year-old Vin Toulson is better known as the "quiet man of the show ring", chalking up 11 hunter championships at Wembley and trophies at every major show, except the Royal Cornwall, but only because he has never been there. The Quiet Man is about to launch two new middleweights, Tom Fir and Casablanca, plus a lightweight, small hunter and young stock on the 1996 circuit, but says starkly: "There has never been a horse to compete with Panhandle's character."

"He would come at you with his mouth open but you could have put your whole hand in and he would not have bitten you. When he won a race he would not load in the trailer; if he lost he would walk straight in."

Vin recalls grumbling to fellow jockey Michael Scudamore as he raced Panhandle round Uttoxeter that he had dropped his whip two fences from home. He beat Michael and Fred Winter by a short head and a neck, and Michael retorted: "I wish you had fallen off with it ..."

Vin chuckles over an embarrassment at Nottingham when Panhandle took his breeches clean off after falling at the last, with the race seemingly in the bag. Although uninjured, the jockey waited for the ambulance to carry him discreetly back to the medical room from where he sent out for a pair of trousers.

But comedy was to turn to tragedy. The winner of five races, Panhandle was now a big talking point in the press, and Vin and the horse swept clear in the King Lear Handicap at Stratford.

But the next morning Panhandle was inexplicably ill and vet Claude Farmer and Vin Toulson fought for a week to save him. It was suggested that Panhandle may have picked up an infection at Stratford, but Vin Toulson said unequivocally: "The horse had been got at, but in those days it was difficult to prove. He was becoming the leading two-mile chaser and was well fancied for the Emblem Chase at Manchester."

Daphne says of Panhandle's loss: "We were heartbroken." Vin agrees: "It seemed as if the bottom had dropped out of our world. I could not believe it and walked around like a zombie for days."

Nearly 40 years on and with hundreds of horses having passed through Gartree Stud, the Toulsons' admiration and affection for Panhandle remain undimmed.

"There has never been another like him," they say in unison.

23 May 1996

The bucking bay who harvested a crop of medals

John Whitaker recalls his glittering 14-year partnership with
Ryan's Son, the show-off show jumper who transformed his life

TUCKED away under John Whitaker's drinks bar in his old stone Yorkshire farmhouse is a box with a chip of bone in it, and precious snippets of mane and tail. They are mementoes of Ryan's Son, the bay horse John's father, Donald, thought was sheer talent and which John, at first sight, considered a cart horse with big feet, big head, too much white on him, a ewe neck and standing barely 16hh.

But in one 24-hour period, Ryan's Son was to become the crucial factor as to whether John Whitaker remained a milkman delivering 40 gallons in pint and half-pint bottles every morning for the family's dairy, or whether he would develop into the sportsman he is today, holder of an MBE, one of the world's greatest show jumpers, with a sackful of medals, and a bag ready to pack for the 1996 Olympics.

Ryan's Son had a mere 50p on his BSJA card when he was given to John by Malcolm Barr, who would later become his father-in-law. The horse and teenager clicked immediately, becoming the team to beat at local shows around Huddersfield.

Then, more ambitiously, the six-year-old Ryan's Son, and John's other horse, Singing Wind, were entered at the Great Yorkshire Show, which posed the stiffest test in their careers. John, at 17, disliked the result, which totalled 20 humiliating faults collected in front of crowds that included former schoolmates, friends and family.

"I was out of my depth," says John, "and I told my father on the way home in the lorry that I did not want to go back to the show the next morning."

Donald Whitaker turned a deaf ear to his son's plea, and the reluctant John and an overly keen Ryan's Son returned to the show the next day to come first in their class, trouncing the teenager's heroes David Broome and Harvey Smith.

"It was unbelievable," says John. "I had looked up to those two all my life, particularly Harvey Smith because he was a Yorkshireman. I had tried to copy what they had done and had been beaten by them. Just one day changes everything in your life. From that point on, I never looked back. Ryan put me on the map, and if it were not for him, I would still be a milkman."

The bay gelding, who resembled a Clydesdale crossed with a Thoroughbred, was on the campaign trail for 14 years, always in the same bit with which he arrived as a four-year-old — a rusty looking twisted snaffle with long cheek pieces, one of which was broken.

He was the biggest money-maker on the circuit for 10 years, an Olympic medallist, and had a posse of fans who adored him for his endearing habit of bucking after the last fence.

"He was showing off," says John. "He knew he had finished by the applause and by feeling me

Cup when Ryan was 17, after the trophy had been snatched from their grasp so many times before. Spot was the last to go in the jump off, and the man who is not renowned for his exuberance, but knowing he had won after touching down over the last, flung his hat high in the air.

Despite a triumph in the Derby, Hickstead was their bogey ground. There, in the early days, Ryan put in a series of uncharacteristic stops and John, exasperated, snatched a branch from a hedge and chastised him for the first and only time.

Hickstead was, in fact, the scene of Ryan's terrible and inconceivable ending. The gelding had a tendency to bank a wide fence by dropping his hind legs in the middle and snatching them up again. In 1987 the 18-year-old Ryan banked the parallel white oxer, failed to snatch his legs in time, and tipped up. It did not seem a bad fall, and horse and rider walked out of the ring.

But three hours later, in a private stable of the master of Hickstead, Douglas Bunn, and with the vet in attendance, Ryan's Son collapsed suddenly and died, probably from an internal haemorrhage.

John and his wife Clare were there, so too was his mother Enid, who had taught John to ride, and father Donald. The family were shocked and in tears.

They covered the gelding with a rug and took snippets of his mane and tail, remembering they still had the tiny chip of bone removed years before in an operation on his pedal bone. The journey back to Yorkshire, without Ryan's Son, who had transformed John Whitaker's life, was the longest, saddest and most silent they ever made.

switch off the pressure. He said: 'That's it, I have done it', and bucked. It was off-putting, though, if the audience clapped after a difficult combination in the middle of a round, because he bucked then too, which would put you wrong for the next fence."

Ryan's only fault was his tendency to hot up and John Whitaker, who is affectionately known as "Spot" to the senior show jumping fraternity, heeded his father's words about not changing tack or tactics, but simply turn Ryan out in the field between shows. It is advice that Spot has followed since with other horses.

"Like the very best of them, Ryan had character, but he was a 'nice person' too. His greatest asset was his consistency. You could guarantee jumping a clear round."

John, 41, who is married with three children, took the odd-looking little Olympian horse around the globe, harvesting silver in the European Championships, and bronze in the World Championships.

But the rider's most treasured moment was capturing the prestigious and elusive King George V

30 May 1996

Charismatic cob who was a cast-iron cert

Trainer John Dunlop recalls his first foray into showing with Just William, twice Cob of the Year and whose good work lived on after his death

WITH a career total of 2,500 exquisite Thoroughbred winners, John Dunlop, Flat racing's champion trainer, drew a deep breath and stared in amazement at his first show horse.

It was the unmade lightweight cob, Just William, looking as bedraggled and unkempt as his namesake from the Richmal Crompton books and, like the fictional character's enemy Violet Elizabeth Bott, John Dunlop could have "scweamed and scweamed".

"He looked the most unprepossessing horse and the most unlikely to become a show horse I had ever seen. I would not have been surprised to have seen him with a chain around his neck and tethered on wasteland outside Slough," he declared.

But the cob and the distinguished governor of Castle Stables in Arundel were standing, in fact, in show doyen Roy Trigg's upmarket Sussex yard.

This was because John had been sending yearlings for Roy and his wife to break and, while visiting in 1984, had admired their top cob, Huggy Bear. John had said offhandedly: "I would rather like a cob sometime."

Today he admits: "Those were fatal words to mention to a horse dealer."

Within the week, Roy Trigg, who died in 1994, was on the telephone offering the bubbly four-year-old, Just William. John Dunlop was happy to buy him over the telephone, but was persuaded to see him and even then was none the wiser.

"I simply had faith in Roy's judgement," he says. That faith has been repaid, for the smartened and

hogged William was Cob of the Year twice in 1989 and 1991, won his class at Wembley four times and chalked up countless championships at the major shows.

"It was like owning a Triple Crown winner," says the trainer. "If we were having a bad week racing, it was marvellous to have Just William land the spoils and give us a bit of a fillip. He was a cast-iron certainty."

The chesnut gelding, who moved more like a hack, was by a Welsh Cob out of a part-Thoroughbred mare, a pussycat in the stables and an enthusiastic ride, but who John Dunlop considered was too sharp for him ever to venture into the saddle.

John never sat on him nor even saw William's Wembley triumph, because the Horse of the Year Show clashes with a busy racing week and the important Houghton sales at Newmarket.

But he had Just William home for the holidays at the end of each season, out in the paddock with splendid views towards the sea and overlooked by the drawing room at the House on the Hill, which was handy for John and his wife Sue to pass sugar lumps and peppermints to their equine pet.

John Dunlop, whose best horses included Shirley Heights, Habibti, Salsabil and Erhaab, saw the equally keen but more chunky William make his debut not far from Epsom, where the trainer has saddled two Derby winners.

The local show venue was in stark contrast — wholly unglamorous — and in a biting wind the champion trainer remembers marvelling at the transformation of his little horse and how he became severely bitten by the showing bug, which has resulted in him sending out a fleet of home-bred young stock and ridden hunter champions.

John recalls seeing William walk on his hindlegs outside the Royal Norfolk ring because he objected to the marching band.

"Not quite the thing for a confidential cob," says his doting owner, "but he never did much wrong, bless him."

While not doing much wrong, the cob was still to cause John Dunlop to smile wryly on two occasions. The first was when William, aged 15, came out of retirement to win at Newmarket's July Jolly, staged for trainers' hacks. The horse he beat that day was called Valentine, who is also owned by John and considered docile enough for him to ride on his Sussex gallops.

The second time William caused an even more serious blip on the trainer's screen occurred after the champion cob had grown cold in his grave.

In the meantime, William was given to the Marchioness of Tavistock, a bloodstock breeder and racehorse owner, who had coveted him after seeing his photograph in *Horse & Hound*.

William joined Lady Tavistock, her stud manager Peter Diamond and his wife Beccy for an action-packed five years at Woburn, primarily as a lead horse for young Thoroughbreds, but also gently carrying the Diamond children, rounding up cattle in the stately park and teaching the Marchioness's younger son his first equestrian skills.

The cob was busy and so keen on arriving anywhere ahead of time that he had to be slowed with a continental gag. They called him the

"Charismatic Cob" and could not decide whether he looked more like a Trojan war horse or a rhino when his hogged mane grew into a crew cut.

"William 'smiled' at you," says Beccy. "He loved life and was so enthusiastic leading young stock that they never thought of napping. The only time William was not foot-perfect was when he passed close to a bison in the safari park and hid behind a yearling."

At the beginning of 1996, Just William, aged 16, contracted colic and died after surgery. Lady Tavistock thought his good work still lived on, but John Dunlop was not so sure.

The reason? Thrilling Day, bred by Lady Tavistock and nannied by Just William, won the Nell Gwyn Stakes at Newmarket, beating the favourite, Bint Salsabil, by a short-head. And Bint Salsabil's trainer? An exasperated John Dunlop, who put it down to a twist of fate.

"William must have had a hand in it," he says, with a wry smile.

6 June 1996

The show-off stallion who loves to strut

Dr Wilfried Bechtolsheimer reminisces about Giorgione, the
dressage star who was responsible for his change of nationality
and could now take him to Atlanta

THE curious fact is that one night German-born Ursula Bechtolsheimer went to bed with her equally German husband and awoke next morning lying happily next to a foreigner.

She was only partly responsible. Mostly it was because of a horse called Gino who, as his nickname suggests, struts like a Latin and whose favourite phrase is "look at me".

It all started when Ursula was courting her husband Wilfried 26 years ago and made it clear she disapproved of his passion for dangerous motor racing.

She introduced him instead to horses. The couple became engaged and received an equine for a present, married, had four children and many more horses, studied under international trainers, three-day evented and then concentrated on dressage.

One of their purchases was the Prix St Georges horse Gino, a 16.3hh Hanoverian stallion registered in 1981 as Giorgione, by Grundstein. He was to go on and carry the youngest British rider ever at the Olympics and now may be bound for Atlanta with the oldest rider on the short-list.

Wilfried saw the chesnut in a Hamburg yard and admits: "It was love at first sight He was vetted, but I had already decided that whatever the vet said, we were going to have him. He had so much power and presence."

Gino, who adores people and has an aversion to cattle, was the big reason why Dr Bechtolsheimer contacted the Home Office and the FEI last year. The former agreed he could become a British

national and the latter said he could compete wearing the British flag. When his new passport dropped on to the mat in July, Ursula, who had gone to bed with a German, was in fact waking up with a Brit.

She sewed the Union Jack on Wilfried's coat and watched as he and Gino won first place in dressage to music at a Hickstead CDI.

"I think the proudest moment of my life was when they played the British National Anthem after our win," says Wilfried.

Now Gino and the doctor, who gave up dentistry to become managing director of his in-laws' business, the German equivalent to Asda with 10,000 employees, are on the British short-list of seven for the 1996 Olympic Games.

"Gino," he says, "sulks if I do not work him and becomes really moody if someone else hacks him out instead of me. It has been a special relationship since the day he arrived. Nothing can touch Gino, not in his performance, way of going, or in the way I feel about him."

Ten years ago, when the hypermarket company went public, the Bechtolsheimers decided to make England home and bought Eastington House and the farm next door, near Cirencester in Gloucestershire.

They built an equestrian centre and Wilfried, who often pilots his executive jet to administer the remaining European businesses of property and hotels, brought in a young German dressage rider to be the stable jockey.

At the time, Wilfried was enjoying training horses and riders and, when his jockey left in 1989, Carl Hester arrived for the job interview.

"I thought, 'My God, he is a little boy'," says the doctor, "but he showed outstanding talent."

The Bechtolsheimers bought Walzertakt for Carl to ride, but the horse turned out to be neither sound nor sane. Swallowing hard, the doctor generously handed Gino over instead, and said: "You have Gino and we will try to get him to Grand Prix standard."

They did better than that — Carl, then aged 25, and the 11-year-old stallion came 17th at the Barcelona Olympics.

"It was a great feeling watching them at the Games," says Gino's proud owner. "I was dying for Carl to pull all the right strings and for Gino to give his best, but my heart was always bleeding a tiny bit, because it was my horse.

"Then there was a bit of an upset when Carl left us in the spring of 1993. I was fed up training young riders who, the minute they knew a bit, left. I said, 'That is it', and started riding myself."

His tail coat from his eventing days came out of mothballs and Dr Wilfried Bechtolsheimer, now 47 and delighted to find it still fitted, went on the road as the Eastington competition rider.

His beloved Gino, though, was left temporarily on the sidelines.

"Everybody had Gino associated with Carl and for me to come out as a newcomer in Grand Prix with the horse would have been stupid. I thought I would wait until I had practised with the others."

Their first competition in 1994 was an embarrassing Intermediaire II when they made a mistake. The doctor halted Gino and did a few unofficial steps of rein back to correct the horse.

Since then, this ardent benefactor of British dressage has scored 11 wins, including nine with Gino, in Grand Prix, and the pair were British team members at the European Championships in Luxembourg.

The bespectacled doctor is amused to think that the horse, who helped spur him into changing countries, having carried the youngest rider at the Olympics, may now carry the oldest on the British short-list.

"If we are not at the Games, it will be disappointing but the world goes on," he says philosophically and then laughs, "Gino would not care a jot. He has already been."

In fact, if horses talked, Gino would elect to stay at home and enjoy a second season covering mares. So far, 14 of his foals have been born this year and glowing reports are coming in from the pleased owners. Most of them have used the same description of Gino's progeny. They say they have his sire's "look at me" presence.

13 June 1996

The pony who talked to his disabled riders

Freckles was one of the Riding for the Disabled Association's truest soldiers – patient, tolerant and caring

WHEN Freckles was buried on the highest point of the cross-country course, he had as many wreaths and bouquets as Red Rum and more precious tears than will probably be shed over Desert Orchid or Milton.

He was a 14.1hh curly-coated gentleman with yobbo tendencies, who never won a thing in his life. He only put his ears forward when he was eating and was a talking horse. Say something to Freckles and he would softly whinny long sentences in reply, even with a mouthful of hay.

His breeding was unknown and while some wits thought he was a short-horn bullock, others reckoned he was by a woolly mammoth out of a Limousin.

Where he originated from, nobody knew. His real history started when he was aged around 11 and the last page was written when he was about 17. Before that he was owned by an assistant instructor, who bought him from a mother with two children who, in turn, it was believed, bought him from a dealer.

Freckles was one of the Riding for the Disabled Association's 4,878 truest soldiers – patient, tolerant and caring.

He would stand dozing by a mounting block while four voluntary helpers eased a stiffened body on to the sheepskin on his back. Then he would walk round the school, giving his riders the only half-hour's freedom they would experience in a week – a chance to look down from Freckles instead of up from their wheelchairs.

Sometimes a child screamed when first on his back, but Freckles would not even flick an ear. Then he would walk on and there would be silence and a look of sheer wonder. The first time one child spoke was to say the word "Freckles".

But give Freckles an able-bodied adult or teenager and he was grease lightning around the cross-country course and when Wendy Murray was mounted on her Thoroughbreds out for a hack, Freckles would overtake, carrying one of her clients, and give her palpitations.

He arrived at Strumpshaw Riding Centre in East Norfolk six years ago looking like an oil barrel on short sticks - a nightmare on which to fit a saddle.

Strumpshaw, with its two indoor schools and an outdoor school, plus 11 acres, is a highly professional establishment where 33-year-old Wendy, the proprietor, puts polish on experienced riders, offers novice children and adults the opportunity of learning the correct way, and gives 100 watt lighting to the disabled in their dark week.

In his early days there, Freckles resembled a Thelwell cartoon character, with riders in danger of slipping around him until he had slimmed down.

"The first time I used him in a lesson he walked into the middle of the school and trod on my foot. I think," says Wendy, whose hours of teaching would have a union in uproar, "he wanted to let me know who was boss."

Freckles worked two hours a day, six days a week with clients like Clare, a Downs Syndrome girl, who considered him her own horse and best friend.

"She used to tell him what she had done at the weekend or what she was having for lunch," says Wendy, "and that horse stood there, and really listened, and then spoke back to her.

"She came to the RDA session after he died and she was sobbing and wanted to cling to me. She could not face getting on another horse."

Wheelchair-bound Jason, who had curvature of the spine, was another big fan of the inimitable strawberry roan. The boy, who has no speech, hummed when he was riding Freckles because he was happy.

"There was a kind of magic between them," Wendy recalls. "Jason loved to touch Freckles and hold his hands close to the horse's nostrils to feel the warmth."

When Freckles died, Jason stopped humming.

Then there was Bob, nothing wrong with Bob – he was aged 80 and asked Wendy one day: "It is a terrible thought that I might pass away without having fulfilled an ambition to ride. Is it too late?"

Bob was able to ride Freckles over a period of three years, cantering around the school and popping cross-poles, until Freckles beat him to the grave. Bob cried, Wendy sobbed, then the livery owners cried and so did each of the clients as they trickled in over the next few weeks and learned the sad news.

Freckles had been the Strumpshaw star, their vaulting horse, boss man out grazing, never kicking or biting but just levelling "The Freckles Look" at another horse, for it to go immediately into reverse. He was the means by which at least a hundred mothers could discipline the disabled or able-bodied children. "Do it," they would say, "or you will not ride Freckles ...". It was a tactic that never failed.

He was not only admired for his kindness, but his cleverness. When Wendy taught able-bodied riders, she would say, for example, "Turn across the school to A" and Freckles was on his way before the rider could ask him. It was a real confidence booster.

The letters were switched to pictures during lessons for the disabled and Wendy could tell Freckles to go and stand at frog, or kangaroo, or elephant, and off he ambled to stand at the correct marker.

Freckles died of a heart attack at 7.30am on April 17 this year. Wendy says: "He knew he was top dog among even the poshest horses in the yard. He gave so much to so many, and we understood each other inside out.

"What I had not realised, though, was how many hearts he had touched. I suppose we were all lucky to have known him."

20 June 1996

The Rolls Royce ride who drove a hard bargain

Jane and Andy Crofts recall the showing career of Periglen
whose impeccable manners and perfect pattern produced so
many wins that he earned a place in the record books

S IXTEEN years ago, at the HIS sales in
Taunton, a mother found the answer to a
perennial question posed to agony aunts about
what to do about the "empty nest syndrome".

The stock reply on a women's magazine problem page tends to run along the lines of "get out
and about and do voluntary work ..." Instead, this
particular mother urged her husband to buy a
horse.

Jane Crofts says the unbroken three-year-old
was a lovely walker and a good mover. Her husband Andy says he exuded quality.

"He was 15.3hh," says Andy.

"Do not exaggerate!" exclaims his wife.

They paid 1,800 guineas for the gelding, gam-
bling that he would make a lightweight hunter, as
he was considered to be "between classes" — too
big for a small hunter, but not tall enough for a
lightweight — and in those days there were no
riding horse classes into which he would have
slotted beautifully.

Showmen David Tatlow and Robert Oliver were
also at the sale, but were not interested in the
horse.

"Robert said afterwards: 'Did you buy that little
horse? He will not be anything.'," says Andy.

The little horse was Periglen, who continued to
grow until the May of his eighth year when he
reached a satisfactory 17½hh, and was considered

to have the perfect pattern. In fact, probationary
judges in the 1980s were urged to seek him out
and study him.

Periglen, by The Ditton, gave Jane Crofts 46 first prizes, 33 championships and six reserve championships at the county shows. He also gave Andy Crofts his first set of dentures after knocking out his three front teeth, not to mention an inordinate amount of satisfaction in being able to remind his old friend Robert Oliver that he had wrongly predicted his little horse's future.

Periglen won more than £3,000 — considered a fortune in showing terms — and set two records at the time by winning the Kent County Show championship four times in a row and by being the first horse to win the East of England's prestigious gold cup three years in succession.

Journalists, who began writing about him in 1981, were running out of accolades by 1985.

"Rolls Royce ride. Unbeatable because of the correctness of his conformation, action and impeccable manners," wrote one show reporter. Another said: "Ultra correct. The outstanding lightweight of the decade. If they decide to send him racing with that gallop, Periglen will bring in a few more wins."

Andy Crofts declares simply: "He was the greatest."

In fact, "Glen", as he was known, marked a new era for the Crofts.

The son of an estate agent and farmer, Andy started working with Sam Marsh's show horses before World War II, first as a schoolboy in the holidays, and then later as his apprentice.

Andy has shown other people's horses all his working life, and was renowned for his expertise with ponies.

Jane, now a grandmother, was also respected for her work with ponies, qualifying for the Horse of the Year Show on numerous occasions as a child, and then finding ponies and schooling them for her daughters, who also competed at Wembley and went on to event.

When the last of the girls flew the nest at Keepers Cottage, which sits in a Surrey wood with six acres, 14 boxes and an outdoor school, the Crofts decided they had the time and freedom to enjoy showing their own horses.

They had dealt in ponies, then hunters and today have changed tack again and specialise in eventers, sending out Alice Clapham, Bridget Enstein and Andrew Nicholson with a string which includes Sky One, Ferndale Charlie Brown and Optimist.

The most reliable horse in their yard, though, for leading young stock and nannying them in the paddocks, is 19-year-old Periglen, showing little wear and tear, and a look that says butter would not melt in his mouth. But it was not always this way with the bay gelding.

"He could be a real 'B'," says Andy. "I remember hacking him out when he was a four-year-old and he would not go down a track for love nor money. I set about him and it was the worst thing I could have done. He was so strong willed. But I had to win. He did not have me off, but he spun and reared, and by the time I arrived home I was pouring with sweat, blood and had lost three teeth. If anybody had offered me £500 for him they could have taken him.

"It was entirely due to Jane's expertise, patience and perseverance that Glen got out of his head-strong ways and became what he was."

Jane explains: "You had to be tactful with Glen and not dominate him. You had to sit on him like a mouse, because if you did not, he would throw in the towel."

As a five-year-old at shows Glen needed lungeing to dampen his short fuse, but despite that he still went into orbit minutes before a Devon County class, and also bucked Jane out of the front door in the Gillingham and Shaftesbury ring.

He was not best behaved indoors either, even though he became an impeccably-mannered gentleman on grass. He was top lightweight twice at Wembley and reserve champion once, but once was enough. The second time under the lights, Periglen became as high as a kite and a judge was heard to remark wryly: "Bang goes our champion".

A prince at the shows, it was almost cruel that he never wore the crown at the Horse of the Year Show. "That was my only disappointment," says Andy.

Jane sums up her showing sojourn with Periglen as "absolutely thrilling", and adds that, "He is part of the family now. We all love him."

Andy and Jane would be extremely happy if they had £1 for every time someone asked them "Could you find us another Periglen?"

4 July 1996

Simply the best — that was the great steeplechaser Arkle

Anne, Duchess of Westminster, recalls the glittering career of Arkle, the show-off racehorse who strode like an emperor and was as brave as a lion

H E was likened to an emperor striding past the post into his empire, leaving his humble subjects huffing and puffing behind him. Someone, considered to be only half joking, wrote the horse's name on a wall in Dublin, with the words "for President" beside it, and envelopes containing his fan mail, scantily addressed with just his name and "Ireland", unerringly arrived.

Betting on him was abnormal — punters merely lent bookmakers their money for 15 minutes, and then received returns slightly higher than the bank rate. It was even rumoured that St Patrick himself regularly backed the horse.

All trainers but his own feared him, and the public, who adored him, flocked to the racetracks. Theorists rowed over him, fiercely debating whether he was the greatest steeplechaser of all time, better than Golden Miller, and faster, because he could have easily switched to Flat racing and won the Cesarewitch under top weight.

His owner, Anne, Duchess of Westminster, busily rushing through life at 81 years old, is in no doubt about his supremacy. Pausing to puff elegantly on a cigarette, she declares with absolute certainty: "Arkle was the most perfect horse the world has ever seen."

The Irish gelding set a UK steeplechase record, running 35 times and winning 27 races, including the Whitbread Gold Cup at Sandown, the King George VI at Kempton, the Hennessy Gold Cup at Newbury, the Irish Grand National, and three Cheltenham Gold Cups in a row — 1964, 1965 and 1966, humiliating Mill House, the English champion.

Arkle also broke course records. He became the fastest three-miler and the most stubborn, because in the 1966 Cheltenham Gold Cup he reached the last fence first time round and struck it, flat out, with his chest. "Then, he went through it like Moses parting the Red Sea," reported a racing journalist. Arkle won at a canter by 30 lengths, the longest distance at the shortest price.

The Duchess first remembers him in 1960 as Lot 148 at Goffs Sales, a three-year-old 16.2hh bay gelding by Archive out of Bright Cherry.

Her trainer, Tom Dreaper, had saddled the dam and the Duchess says: "I liked the breeding, particulary the bottom line."

She looked over him, ignored a long scar, bought him for 1,150 guineas, and went on to win first prize-money of £75,107 3s.

Arkle's breeding was only interesting because of a coincidence that was discovered later. Both sides of his pedigree traced back to Bend Or, the first Duke of Westminster's racehorse who triumphed in the 1880 Derby. That Duke's grandson became the second Duke who, at 68 years old and

reputedly one of the richest men in Britain, married his fourth wife, now Anne, Duchess of Westminster.

The Duchess was neither interested in Arklemania nor the prize-money, which was a record-breaking amount. First and foremost she was a horsewoman, a brigadier general's daughter who rode across Irish and English foxhunting country as unswervingly as the crow flies.

Speaking at her home in Eaton Lodge, Chester, where a corridor is lined with Arkle's pictures and ornaments of him cast in clay, bronze and china, she says: "He was as brave as a lion, always with his ears pricked, and a tremendous show off in front of the crowds."

She admired Arkle's prowess in public, but loved him best in private as the horse who liked to roll in his box, as many as a dozen times in one session, and who would come home to her stud farm for a holiday at the end of each season.

There, he would gallop across a field to her for sugar and, if he was lying down in the field or box, would not bother getting up, but allow her to sit with him, resting his head in her lap. "I felt I could talk to him," she says.

She would get him ready to go back into training by riding him around the farm, finding that the speed merchant who could leap 7ft over a fence could also be a placid gentleman at canter and patient while she opened and closed gates.

From 1961, when Arkle first unfurled his racecourse banners, the Duchess, who always wore her lucky brooch while he was running, never watched him jump a final fence and only looked up when she knew he was safely past the post. She resisted pressure too, from the trainer, plus the legendary 6ft-tall jockey, Pat Taffe, the punters and the press to run Arkle in the Aintree Grand National.

"I was not prepared to risk him because I adored him — he was one of the family, and far too precious. He would have jumped it perfectly but I was frightened that he would be brought down by loose horses or those refusing in front of him," she says.

On December 27, 1966, Arkle lined up for his second crack at the King George VI at Kempton. Woodland Venture and Dormant took him on from the start, six fences out Arkle made a mistake, and Woodland Venture took over the lead.

Arkle fought back for his rightful place. It seemed impossible that he could lose, but Dormant caught him and passed him in the final 50 yards. Everyone's astonishment turned to disbelief because Arkle, who pulled up lame, had run his heart out despite a fractured pedal bone.

He was in plaster until the following February when, still in pain, he went home to the Duchess at Co Kildare, where she retired him.

"He became stiff, as great athletes do when they are not in work," she says. "One day, I went out to the box and he could not get to his feet. There was nothing for it but to put him down."

Arkle was 13, and the Duchess adds: "I did not want him to suffer. I am not a great weeper but I think I cried when I said goodbye to him."

11 July 1996

The pint-sized Olympian who loved the crowds

Mark Todd recalls an emotional partnership with Charisma,
the diminutive powerhouse who carried him to two individual
Olympic gold medals

WHAT would give one person a nervous breakdown would merely give Mark Todd slight agitation.

He is cool, courageous and, apart from a couple of months in 1984, has gone through his 40 years smoothly, efficiently and unruffled, much the same way as he has harvested two individual Olympic gold medals and three Badminton trophies.

But those few months in 1984 saw Mark the most agitated he has ever been, making anxious transatlantic telephone calls and being too restless to sleep.

It should have been party time for this Kiwi, rated the greatest event rider of his generation. Instead he returned triumphant from the Los Angeles Games where he rode Charisma, to find Charisma's owner dropping a bombshell. She was selling the horse and banning Mark from buying it.

"She was determined there was no way I was going to have Charisma," he exclaims, "and to this day I do not know why."

Mark, who had a sponsor willing to pay the £50,000, was sickened to his stomach and the language he uses about that owner, even now 12 years later, would shock sensitive ears.

But he and the former British team rider Lizzie Purbrick formed a devious plan. Lizzie told Charisma's owner that her husband Reggie want-

ed to buy the horse for her as a spectacular birthday present. She laughs about it today and says, "We could hardly afford to shoe it, let alone buy it".

So, secretly, Mark's sponsor's money went into the Purbricks' bank, straight out again to Charisma's owner, and the brown Thoroughbred gelding went home to Mark. The threat to sue and rows which followed are another story.

"Charisma is very special, not only because of what he has achieved," stresses Mark, "but because he is lovely to have around."

In one of those quirky coincidences, Mark Todd saw Charisma as a three-year-old in 1975 when the horse was turned out on the farm where Mark was working, milking cows.

The 6ft 3in lanky dairyman with ambitions to be a professional rider remembers looking at the 15.3hh gelding and thinking: "Cute. What a shame he will not be big enough".

Eight years later, the little and large duo were brought together by a public relations officer for New Zealand's horse trials. "There is this horse called Charisma," she said. "Do you want to have him for the season?"

Mark, unimpressed by the fat, hairy pony, but reckoning it would be fun, proceeded to win everything on the agenda, four one-day events, the national one-day championship and the national three-day championship.

Then, the relatively inexperienced partnership flew to England to tackle the 1984 Badminton.

Mark recalls the horse, now nicknamed Podge for his gargantuan appetite, approaching Badminton's footbridge, taking off on a long stride, clearing the fence like a fighter jet, and landing far out the other side.

"He had tremendous scope," he says.

Despite coming an easy second there, Mark still thought it necessary to seek out maestro Ted Edgar's advice on show jumping.

"Podge was a cunning old ratbag," complains the Kiwi. "He would jump like a show jumper at Ted's and revert back to his normal self in competition, doing it by 'braille method'. In the end, I left the job up to Podge. He knew just how much he had to give."

Little and large won gold in Los Angeles and retained the precious metal in Seoul, where their dressage was rated more technically correct than the winner of the Grand Prix Special at the same Olympics.

"He was only one of two inside the time across country, making it feel like a Pony Club track and although he had a fence down in the show jumping," says Mark, "Charisma won comfortably."

But between those Olympic golds, the duo had their ups and downs. At one three-day event, Podge blew up in the dressage, ran away with Mark in the cross-country, and had five fences down in the show jumping.

"He was taking the mickey," declares Mark, "and at that time in his life, if he did not have a large enough audience, he would not bother. He won the next time out at Gatcombe and possibly one of the reasons was that they had bigger attendances."

At 16, Charisma was retired to Mark's property in New Zealand to be cared for by the farm manager, allowed out hunting only once because of his madcap behaviour and becoming a New Zealand superstar, the Kiwi equivalent of Desert Orchid and Red Rum.

"Seoul was wonderful," Mark says, "but one of the most proud and moving moments of my career was riding Charisma into the stadium at Auckland, under a spotlight, to open the World Games."

It brought a lump to his throat and he felt equally emotional earlier this year when Charisma stepped off a plane in England.

For Mark Todd, who is bound for Atlanta and not looking forward to it because of the toll the climate could exact from the horses, finally sold his New Zealand property and, instead of renting other people's stables in this country, put down roots in a Cotswold stone farmhouse.

Charisma joined him, his wife Carolyn and their two children and the first guest invited to ride the horse was Lizzie Purbrick who had "bought" him unseen back in those troubled days of 1984.

"Charisma carted me across the field and Mark was laughing so much he could hardly watch," says Lizzie, declaring, "he is one of the strongest horses I have ever ridden."

At 24 years old, the pint-sized Olympian equine is sound, supple and as onward-bound as ever. Mark reports: "He still goes better than half the horses in the yard, jumps superbly and can do two-time flying changes. In fact, when he arrived here, he was wondering for a whole week whether he was back in training or not."

Mark pauses and looks at Charisma as if seeing him for the first time again.

"He is so tiny," he says incredulously. "I wonder how he achieved so much. He is such a sweet horse. I owe it to him to look after him in his retirement."

18 July 1996

The pocket-sized pony who was a jewel of a show jumper

Marion Mould reminisces about winning silver at the Mexico
Olympics on Stroller

IT was a fairy tale that descended to a horror story. In a mere four days, she reached the pinnacle of the whole world cheering at her, only to fall to the depths of being shunned by her team mates.

At 21, Marion Coakes and her phenomenal 14.2hh pony Stroller, with quarters better suited to a 16.2hh horse, won the individual silver medal at the Mexico Olympics on a sunny Wednesday in 1968, becoming the blonde heroine and the pocket-sized bay hero of the crowds and television viewers around the globe.

The following Sunday, Marion rode Stroller from the warm-up area through the tunnel and entered the same arena for the team event. But this time she sensed that Stroller was not feeling 100 per cent and that perhaps she should not be there at all. The tunnel seemed to go on for miles and to engulf her completely.

The deafening applause that met her was soon replaced by shocked cries and a deafening silence, for the pair was about to give the worst performance in its sensational career. Rider and pony cleared the wall, only to crash to the ground at a parallel.

"I remember Stroller on the floor and that I had banged my head," says Marion. "The next thing I can recall is walking out of the arena with Harvey Smith waving his arms, saying, 'Get back in'.

"But it was too late and the team was eliminated, because in those days there were only three in a team and each score counted.

"It was horrific," she says with a shudder. "I felt sick. I had gone from being in the highest esteem to the lowest and all I wanted to do was get out of the place."

She telephoned her boyfriend, now her husband — David Mould — who was the Queen Mother's National Hunt jockey, for comfort. Later, in her British athlete's uniform, Marion walked alone in the Games' closing parade — "the team had disappeared".

That winter was extremely bleak as Marion considered that she and the pony had not merely been written off, but chewed up and spat out. Stroller had an operation on a tooth and his sinuses, while Marion moped.

Only seven years previously, the highly gifted 14-year-old rider had spotted Stroller at Chichester Show.

"Stroller looked fabulous," she recalls, "and utterly brilliant. He came up for sale after the Horse of the Year Show for £1,000 and the first time that I sat on him was when we went to pick him up from a field behind a butcher's shop. We were meant to be together, but nobody realised how much potential he had."

A year later in the school holidays Marion jumped for Britain in the junior team, and in the

winning Nations Cup teams.

By the time she was 21, Marion had written six books and travelled the world, not to mention the superstar status that she and Stroller revelled in during the sport's heyday. Now 49, Mrs Marion Mould does not even have a passport, content to stay at home with David, who tips racehorses for *Daily Mail* readers under the *nom de plume* of "Gimcrack", and their seven-year-old son Jack, in a cottage near Lymington, named The Strollers.

Recently, they watched some videos of Marion and Stroller.

"I cannot believe we actually did all that," she says.

"Stroller achieved so much, but more than that, he was my friend, my best buddy with whom I could sit and talk in the stable. We had a relationship from day one."

It was her loyalty to the pony which roused her after the Mexico débâcle and long, grim winter, to come out of hibernation and prove they were not washed up.

Horse and rider contested the 50th Hamburg Derby, where they were the first to go of 35 riders and jumped the only clear round to receive a standing ovation.

following year was competing nine-year-old Stroller in senior classes.

It was as easy as shelling peas for the formidable duo. He was quiet, easy, and laid back, while his partner exuded confidence and a fierce will to win.

They hardly practised over fences, mostly going for hacks down to the Hampshire beach, overlooking the Isle of Wight, to canter along the sands.

For six years, between 1964 and 1970, the jumping machine and girl rider won 61 international competitions, including the Hickstead Derby, two Ladies' World Championships, the Queen Elizabeth II Cup twice, the Leading Show Jumper Of The Year title and the pair also shone in five

They won their last class at Wembley where Stroller was retired, aged 20 or 21 — Marion cannot remember which.

It was a wet day on 24 March 1986 and Marion's equestrian centre was unusually quiet. She telephoned her parents Ralph and Olive Coakes to say she was coming over for lunch. As soon as she arrived, Stroller became unwell and a few hours later had a heart attack.

"It was so moving," says Marion. "I'm sure he had waited for me so I could say goodbye to him.

"I think that I had the closest relationship with Stroller that anyone could have with a horse or pony," she says.

25 July 1996

The manic mare who led the way with courage

Liz Finney recalls Showgirl's medal-laden endurance career
and how horse and rider thought with one mind

THE mare totally lost her head at the European Championships when she considered the temporary stable too small for comfort.

Showgirl lay flat, burrowing her head under the canvas partition, and when her rider came to check on her, she found an equine torso. But intruding and snoozing in the next door stable were Showgirl's head and neck, while the indignant and rightful occupant stood quivering and snorting, pressed against the wall.

It was obvious that Showgirl could relax and conserve energy under the most trying of circumstances and this was one of the reasons why she is Britain's biggest success in endurance riding.

The sport is today's appliance of equestrian science — the equivalent of the great horse journeys of the past, by the Pony Express in the Wild West; Black Bess, who sped from London to York to provide Dick Turpin with an alibi; and the horses in Genghis Khan's dispatch service, whose messengers were executed if they lost time.

Death was exactly what Showgirl's owner, Cath Kennedy, felt like after she watched the daisy fresh, dark brown mare complete, in spectacular fashion, the first 100-mile Golden Horseshoe Ride in 1986, only to be eliminated because Showgirl's pulse rate was 68, when the rule states that it should not rise above 64.

After that, Showgirl's pulse rate was as steady and reliable as Big Ben, and of a record-breaking nine consecutive attempts at this Exmoor challenge, Showgirl picked up six gold and two silver awards.

The exuberant mare was in three European Endurance Championships, winning a bronze medal with Cath's eldest daughter Andrea, and partnering Cath's friend Liz Finney, a pharmacist, to chalk up an individual silver and team silver.

But in the 1990 World Equestrian Games in Stockholm, where 60 riders lined up for a 100-mile race across heart-stopping country, Showgirl, although collecting a team gold, was showing off and fell 10 miles from the finishing line.

"She was in season," says Liz, "and we had this French stallion up our back end for most of the way."

Now 20 years old, Showgirl has a total of 64,000 miles on her clock, 6,400 of them in competition, resulting in only a couple of windgalls, and hefty bills for new sets of reinforced shoes every fortnight.

This granddaughter of Quorum, who sired Red Rum, was the largest horse in her sphere, a Goliath among Davids. Looking more like a show hunter, she was originally aimed at riding club events, only coming to endurance because it made economic sense.

Cath Kennedy, a 52-year-old grandmother, paid £600 for the mare for Andrea, and was promptly bucked overboard when Showgirl arrived at their Cheshire home.

The new purchase was nicknamed "Short Straw", because anyone who rode the bronco had drawn the short straw, but that name was quickly upgraded to "Kali", the Indian goddess who had a taste for blood.

Endurance riding was in its infancy at the time and appealed to Cath and Andrea.

"You get a lovely countryside, a super long ride and your horse vetted," says Cath.

"Kali" was soon entered for long-distance rides, and they discovered that after the first 20 miles her manic behaviour, which has included rolling in mud, getting up and breaking two of Andrea's ribs with a full velocity kick, gradually settled, and that she also had an automatic gear box.

Liz Finney, who partnered the mare to international success, says Showgirl was "amazing. She did it all with the minimum of effort. She seemed to switch off mentally, settle into a rhythm and keep travelling.

"I felt I did not need to ride her, just guide her, and sometimes I did not even have to do that, because she understood the flags, tapes and arrows on the ground. She has whipped me round a corner many times in competition and I have asked, 'Where are we going?' and then spotted the marker. She knew exactly what she was doing."

Showgirl, who always wriggled out of her British team rugs and piled them in a stable corner, and whinnied when she spotted her "crew" bringing up electrolyted refreshments en route, was "remarkable for her courage, stamina and incredible soundness," says Liz.

She brought Cath undreamed of success and, in return, "Kali" has received slave-like devotion.

She brought Liz a deep understanding of endurance race-riding, and the reality of something she had only read about — a horse and rider who are entirely thinking with one mind.

Liz is now chairman of the BHS Endurance Riding Group and *chef d'équipe* to the British team bound for Kansas to contest the World Endurance Riding Championship on 21 September.

Today Showgirl is "retired", and only does "short trips" of 50 miles. She was powering through Delamere Forest in Cheshire recently with a new jockey, watched by Cath, accompanied by Liz, mounted on a seven-year-old.

"She looked fantastic," says Liz, "just like the early days, ears pricked and travelling."

In fact the old mare was leading the way — as usual.

1 August 1996

The "odd couple" who made a perfect match

Tandem driver Tommy Fawcett recalls triumphant wins with saintly Sam and flamboyant Alfie, his dynamic duo

WHILE the readers of *Horse & Hound* were highly amused at the Christmas caption competition, the subjects of the picture could also see the funny side.

The cameraman had caught the Danish dog cart as it toppled over, Barbara Fawcett in mid-air, her husband Tommy in flight too, about to crack a couple of ribs, and their tandem horses Sam and Alfie reacting as per usual.

That meant Alfie, the leader who had caused the spill, was ready to quit the grounds of Lowther Castle and bolt as far south as Watford Gap, and Sam the wheeler, sweet dependable Sam, digging in his feet and stifling a yawn.

"All his life," says Tommy Fawcett, "Sam has had to put up with Alfie."

If Sam and Alfie had been human they would have made a team of detectives. Sam, the good guy, would have operated with painstaking attention to detail, offering tea and a cigarette to a suspect being questioned.

Alfie, his partner, would have been the bad guy, a chancer, occasionally showing shades of brilliance and ready to beat a confession out of the suspect.

Back in the 1980s this odd couple of Welsh Cobs were never boring Mr Plods of horse driving, winning the National Horse Tandem Championship twice, and standing triumphant in 10 other competitions.

Tommy Fawcett, their celebrated whip and now *chef d'équipe* to the British four-in-hand team, says Sam and Alfie's success was certainly due to

"opposites always making the best match".

There would have been more glory if Alfie had always stuck to the rule. Legend has it that an ecstatic woman at Scone Palace watched Sam and Alfie perform a superlative dressage test, and cruise through the cross-country. She then phoned her mother to warn her to attend Tatton Park in Cheshire, to witness the incomparable pair a month later.

The mother thought her daughter was deranged, because all she saw was a snorting Alfie, with tail erect, drag the vehicle, Sam and a protesting Tommy into the arena, and rear throughout the dressage. The cross-country was only remarkable because Alfie shied and danced away from the hazards.

"When Alfie was good, he was excellent," says Tommy. "When Alfie was bad, he was just Alfie. Sam, on the other hand, was always a saint."

Tommy Fawcett, now 54, with three children, farms 250 acres on the edge of the Lake District, only four miles from his friend, leading carriage driver George Bowman, who likes his horse teams to be colour co-ordinated.

George had bought Sam as a foal, had broken him to ride and drive at three, but as a rich chestnut with four white socks and a flaxen mane and tail, he was a total mismatch in George's liver chesnut period.

He sent him to the Fawcetts for Barbara to ride, and then her husband took him over to learn to drive. Tommy and the steady, obliging, tolerant cob came last in their first three competitions, and

won their fourth. At five years old, Sam was the Single Horse National Champion.

"He was a proper little hero," says Tommy. "We had a special relationship."

Tommy, though, was anxious for a greater challenge, something equally economical. He chose the tandem, requiring only one more horse and an extra bit of harness. The sport is rated the most precise and difficult of all on the driving circuit.

In 1979, eight-year-old Enstone Alfie, a £1,000, 15.3hh liver chesnut Welsh Cob arrived on the scene, exuding pride, flamboyance and extravagant paces.

"It was like putting Alfie's V8 engine in Sam's Morris Minor," recalls Tommy. "Alfie was trouble. Suddenly, I had to shout and crack my whip, and Sam, trundling along as calmly as usual, thought, 'What the hell is going on here?'

"Within three months they were blood brothers. Sam would knock a stable door or gate to bits if Alfie was taken away from him, and Alfie would pine and not eat if Sam was separated from him."

Their success or failure in competition was often at the whim of Alfie, whose antics turned the vehicle over three times. But they went on to bring fame to Tommy Fawcett, not as much for his undeniable skills, or his contribution to the Horse Driving Trials Group committee, or even his role as *chef d'équipe*. For, from the Midlands to Massachusetts, driving fans would shake Tommy's hand and say the same four words: "Ah, Sam and Alfie".

Today, while Tommy brings two Lusitanos onto the driving circuit for the first time, the "odd couple" are retired, contentedly grazing in a three-cornered field with a stream running through it.

It is across the road from Tommy and Barbara who check on them twice a day. Sam, 24, and Alfie, 25 are side by side, "so close it would be difficult to slide a piece of paper between them," says Tommy.

The bright bay who banked on putting Red Rum in the shade

Trainer "Ginger" McCain recalls how he is still haunted by
memories of Honeygrove Banker who had the potential to win
every racing honour

TRAINER Donald "Ginger" McCain could not bring himself to bin the cherished record cards, even though the horse had been dead for years.

Not the record cards of his three times Grand National winner Red Rum, but those of Honeygrove Banker, the bright bay gelding who haunts him like an unfinished symphony. Even today as he breaks in eight newcomers at his 200-acre farm in Cholmondeley, Cheshire, Ginger McCain, 65, casts an expert eye and asks: "Is there another Banker among them?

"Red Rum was a one-off, a dour professional and a survivor. The Banker had class," he declares with emphasis.

Honeygrove Banker had more than that, he had an unlimited potential and Ginger McCain reckoned he could be the aspiration of his dreams, his Champion Hurdler and Cheltenham Gold Cup horse.

The ebullient trainer found the horse after both had been much travelled. The unbroken four-year-old Banker had been in and out of auctions in Ireland and England before Ginger paid 4,400 guineas for him at Doncaster in 1985 and received a tirade of abuse from his assistant trainer, Beryl, also his wife, because they could not afford him.

"I am a dealing man so any day I do not have a deal is a bad day. The Banker was the deal I could not pass by. He had size, quality and presence."

The 16.3hh gelding by Cawston's Clown was to give Ginger McCain the tingle factor.

He and his pals had a gamble on the Banker, when he made his debut at Uttoxeter in a two mile novice hurdle with Jonjo O'Neill in the plate.

Ginger chuckles as he recalls how his chum Alan Orrit confidently rushed away to order six bottles of champagne as the Banker took the lead coming into the straight, with two more still to jump.

The trainer wrote the race details on a record card, summing up the win in only two words, the first of which rhymed with hissed, and the second was up.

A week later, Banker and Jonjo were repeating their success at Haydock.

Then trouble loomed in a hot hurdle race at Doncaster where he stood off the second last, clipped it and fell. "He was on the floor for a bit and I felt sick. I was completely in love with the horse and thinking the sky was the limit."

Ginger McCain was concerned by the Banker's muddle over hurdles but not overtly worried. He had been schooled over fences and could measure them better.

In the meantime, the gentlemanly Banker was kept to hurdling, running four more times at top weight, picking up a second, a third and a win and was given rest at grass. He came back to the track again like a cheetah, sprinting 20 lengths ahead in the Captain Quist at Kempton.

It was to cost dearly. He suffered tendon trouble, resulting in 18 months off work, which put paid to a £100,000 offer for him from the British Bloodstock Agency.

There was also discord among his owners and the Banker was sent to Ascot Sales, only to return home again to a delighted Ginger, when he failed to reach his reserve.

On 16 April 1988, however, the horse was fit and harmony was back in the camp. Running in bandages and a little "ring rusty", the Banker came third at Ayr. A week later, the ascending equine star lined up at Uttoxeter in what was meant to be his last hurdle race before graduating to fences.

"He was in tremendous form. I was tickled pink and full of him," says Ginger.

Honeygrove Banker cruised into the lead, stood too far off a hurdle and fell, breaking his neck. He was dead in the time it took Ginger McCain to lower his binoculars.

Today, Ginger shakes his head and says: "He was as fit as 10 fleas one minute and gone the next. It is a man's sport and you know these things happen but it does not make it any easier."

The Banker's stable lass Lesley Rimmer was sobbing and the trainer grimaced in pain as he was handed back the tack but no horse.

Ginger McCain was to go on to pay the greatest compliment to the horse by buying the Banker's half-brother Tribal Ruler, who may run in the Grand National next year. "He is not as good as the Banker, though," he says.

"The Banker's tragedy was that he never realised his potential. I cannot forget him because there is always the unanswered question: 'How good would he have been?'

"More than that, I loved him. You could go into his box at night and just stand looking at him because he filled the eye."

Sadly, one of the last sentences written about Honeygrove Banker in the form book before he died, said it all.

"Should win more races."

15 August 1996

113

Monty's pint-size partner with the heart of a giant

Master horseman Monty Roberts describes his magical
relationship with Peppernick's Dually, who became the love
of his life

MARVIN "MONTY" ROBERTS, the "horse
whisperer" who "gentles" horses not
"breaks" them, was seven years old when his
father grabbed a chain from a stable doorway and
viciously beat him.

"He was brutal towards me, other people and
animals. I loathed him," says Monty candidly,
"and loathed the way he worked his horses.

"The one thing I have to thank him for is that he
swung the pendulum so far in pain and restraint,
that I had to bring it back, and devote my life to
apologising to the equine species."

Now 61, Monty Roberts, whose advance, retreat
and join up technique, which, once used on a wild
horse, can have him peacefully ridden in 30
minutes, has gone a stage further in kindness to
equines, with an experiment.

The result is Peppernick's Dually, "Doolly" for
short, named after an American truck, and who
can be ridden without a bridle.

Doolly was picked as the experiment's guinea
pig, for despite being bred in the purple of
Western performance horses, Monty reckoned he
needed culling.

"He was a weird little guy, so short you
cannot ride him through tall grass. I thought
'Here is our horse for finding out how much
animation, agility, speed and spirit can be
created for work without spurring and jerking.

We will ride him using only leg aids.'"

A cheerful chap with not an unkind thought,
Doolly made early training hazardous, as, deaf to
voice and unused to leg aids, he could be half a mile
from his stable and take three hours to return home.

At four years old, the sturdy 14.3hh bay won the
Triple Crown at the US Reined Cow Horse
Association's national competition — the
cowboy's Olympics — which involves dressage
movements and the sorting of cattle.

Unlike the other competitors, Doolly can go into
a herd with his rider, but without his bridle, cut
out a designated cow and keep it from rejoining
the others. He can also pirouette, gallop and come
to a halt.

But the experiment produced something else —
an extraordinary bond grew between Doolly and
the man who thought there was no use for him, as
he was such an ugly duckling.

"He is the most intelligent and incredible little
horse," says Monty. "He is the love of my life and
closer to me than most of the kids I have raised."

Monty Roberts and his wife Patricia, who have
been married for 40 years, have three children of
their own and have fostered another 47.

It is open house on their 200-acre Californian
farm near Santa Barbara, where, recently, 180
came to dinner in the Roberts' 50 foot cavernous
kitchen.

Sixty of the 250 horses on the farm are Monty's, and there is a staff of 28 — five manning the offices and organising Monty's dizzying diary of worldwide engagements.

But what the softly-spoken horseman likes best is walking with Doolly through the pasture, the little horse following freely and magically as if connected by invisible string, or their rides into the hills, where Monty dismounts, and Doolly watches him play advance and retreat with the wild deer.

They sometimes cut cattle at neighbouring farms or venture further afield to the tranquillity of the mountains.

Monty is proud of Doolly.

"He is a world-class athlete without pain or restraint, but not without discipline. He has been brought along in a different way from any other horse, and everything he does is because he wants to do it."

Now a six-year-old, Doolly is about to become famous as he features in Monty's book, *The Man Who Listens To Horses*, which will be published on 26 September, and is also the star of Monty's 15-venue British tour from 24 September–27 October.

"The jockey Willie Carson once said to me that I do a lot of good among horses, but that I did not understand a horse's mouth. I am inviting him to ride Doolly. Willie will feel velvet," promises Monty. "The horse is phenomenal."

Adds the horse whisperer: "He is the horse I have come to know late in life, when there are no pressures. He has my complete and utter devotion, and I have his. It works both ways."

12 September 1996

The Romeo who stole everyone's heart

Showman Bill Bryan recalls his charismatic soul mate, Romeo,
the noble grey gelding who gave him the ultimate prize —
Hunter of the Year at Wembley

IT is easy to imagine showman Bill Bryan as aloof and hard on his horses when he declares adamantly: "I do not make a pet, or a fool of a horse, as my granddaughter does of a dog, by cuddling him."

Bill Bryan, though, has sacked grooms for striking a horse in his box, and he has been as emotional over one particular equine as any simpering female muttering soppy sentiments and planting kisses on her horse's head.

A discreet tear crept down Bill's face when he won Wembley's Hunter of the Year title, not only because he had waited half a lifetime for the ultimate prize at the Venue of Legends, but because Romeo was his passion.

This noble grey gelding, who needed six bags of housewives' Dolly Blue to bring out the white in him and then when clean, liked to roll, even on bare concrete, was never interested in captivating the one girl in the balcony, but whole audiences.

He and Bill were soul mates. They hated holidays, got carried away when hounds spoke and lived for their jumping.

"He was just like a Bryan," says Bill, "mad for jumping and always wanting to be busy."

When Bill was 12, he hunted a pony or a mule with the North Warwickshire, sometimes having to use a piece of sacking instead of a saddle. As a young man with his own establishment at Kinnesley, Herefordshire, he hunted with three packs, trained point-to-pointers, exhibited show horses, and supported the local hunter trials. Romeo slotted the grey gelding into this bustling

business as if he had been tailor made for it.

Bill spotted the four-year-old gelding by a French Thoroughbred in 1962 at Ascot Sales, where he bucked off the vendor's lad.

"I squared him up, got £5 for schooling him and then bought him for £800."

They hunted that season and, on one heady day, jumped three five-bar gates and smashed up a fourth, for which Bill had to compensate the farmer.

Next, Romeo ran in two point-to-points, coming third and fourth, and went straight on to the show circuit.

Five months later, they captured the supreme hunter title at the Horse of the Year show, retained it in 1964, were reserve champions in 1965 and had a near miss, too, in the workers, when Romeo jumped a stile and, before Bill could turn him, had swept through eight feet of brush, which was there for design and not meant to be jumped.

Romeo's owner Mrs Pam Morris rejected £6,000 for the horse which was offered in one of the Wembley bars and the hopeful purchaser was so piqued he smashed his whisky tumbler on the floor and stormed out.

Romeo returned to the hunting field with a delighted Bill, who decided to campaign the gelding in point-to-points.

"We had Robin Knipe on him in the four-mile Crudwell Gold Cup and Romeo jumped the most boldly I have seen. He took it up after three miles, one came up to challenge him and then another. He out-galloped them all, with ears pricked the whole way. He was like a tank rolling on regardless of the enemy."

Romeo, who won 15 races, was too elegant to be described as an Army vehicle. He was a 16.3hh middleweight with a stupendous gallop, a comfy dip in his back in which to place the saddle and a luxurious length of rein. He was in constant need of a good farrier because of his flat feet and corns.

Bill, a 67-year-old grandfather held in affection by showing afficionados, and who is now bound for Wembley 1996 with his former heavyweight winner Showman, says fondly of Romeo: "He made riding and training worthwhile.

"He had charisma in the ring, would go as fast or as slow as you liked, do what you wanted, cross the most difficult country and never give up or be tired.

"One of the Masters of the South Hereford said Romeo was 'the best ride, and the bravest' he had met, and I had to agree with him. I respected that horse more than any other. I never made a pet of him, but I was fond of him."

Romeo, pottery on his feet and unable to hunt, was put down when he was 14 and buried on a stretch of Bill Bryan's property called No Man's Land.

With five of his six children and six grandchildren riding regularly, Bill says there is never room for him in the manege. He wants to build another to give to the family and the ideal spot is on top of Romeo's burial ground.

"Not only would he not mind," says Bill, "but I think Romeo would approve."

26 August 1996

The "smashing" show jumper who popped Puissance walls

Course-builder and former show jumper Alan Oliver recalls
his legendary 22-year partnership with Red Admiral, the
gentle chesnut who won all the top prizes

ALAN OLIVER looked as though he had returned from the Somme instead of the hunting field. Visibly shaking and coated in mud and blood, the teenager stood in front of his father.

"How did the new horse go?" he asked unnecessarily.

"I jumped six fences and had five falls," replied Alan being economic with the truth as he and the Thoroughbred had, in fact, approached six fences, and smashed through them, not over them.

The Olivers had already been warned by the frank and genuine vendors at Leicester Sales that nobody would ever make the four-year-old gelding into a jumper, but Phil Oliver ignored them and successfully bid 160 guineas.

"We'll try him over a few coloured poles instead," said Phil, ushering Alan, still in hunting kit, outside for schooling.

Six years later, Alan and the Thoroughbred, named Red Admiral after the butterfly which fluttered past his rider's nose, were on the short-list for the Olympic Games in Helsinki.

"Addie", who had originally arrived with a "does not jump" label, was the 1953 Leading Show Jumper of the Year, twice National champion, three times victor of the Horse of the Year Show's Puissance, and had a place in the winning British team for the Nations Cup at the Royal International.

But they had their finest moments in the 1954 drama for the King George V Trophy watched by a nation glued to their black and white television sets. The jumps were continually raised for five long rounds as Alan and Addie fought it out with Fritz Thiedemann and Meteor for Germany, until the British pair clipped the last fence.

It caused such a sensation that Alan was on the news and invited to talk about it on the *In Town Tonight* programme.

The 5ft 9ins, slightly-built rider, with an unorthodox style in the saddle, who point-to-pointed, raced under Rules, and show jumped more rounds than any other British competitor, now erects fences as an advanced course builder.

The 64-year-old was at Towerlands building a

Newcomers' course reflecting his heady days with Red Admiral: "He was the worst hunter I ever rode, and an 'ordinary' horse at a country show, but give him a big audience and atmosphere and he was sensational. You could ride him down to a 7ft 3in wall and he would pop over.

"Mind you," he adds, "you could not get him in deep at his fences. He had to stand off and have a cut at them."

The 16.1hh chesnut with four white legs was so sweet and gentle he could be trusted with riders of any ability, which was useful as Alan Oliver had a big string on the circuit, including Sweep and Pitz Palu, but no groom. He would collar a show jumping fan around the collecting ring, and put them on Addie to walk round for half an hour.

"Once I heard a terrible scream," he says, "and thought, 'My God' what's happened?' I rushed over and found Addie had snatched a child's ice cream and eaten it."

The bond between them was so strong that Alan could whistle him up across a showground, he would ignore who was riding him, and trot over.

There was, however, someone else to whom Addie was equally devoted. This was Red Star, an Irish horse who was the same age, bought at the same time and who was stabled beside him at the Olivers' farm near Aylesbury, Bucks.

When one was taken to a show, the other, who was left behind, called and box walked until his friend returned. Tired of the disturbances, Phil Oliver eventually told his son: "In future take both of the b*****s with you."

The pair were on the circuit for 22 seasons until they retired aged 26. They grazed side by side for three more years, then the snows came and Phil decided it would be kindest to put them down.

He waited until Alan had gone hunting and had the horses dispatched within minutes of each other.

"I lost a friend that day," says Alan. "Addie and I grew up together. He launched my career and gave me the thrill of riding him. Addie was the kindest horse," he stresses, "that anybody ever sat on."

3 October 1996

The "useless" racehorse who pipped the Prince at the post

TV racing presenter Derek Thompson recalls how "no-hoper" Classified helped him with his dream win on the Flat and went on to come third in the Grand National

FEELING uncomfortably nervous, television racing presenter Derek Thompson was grappling with Classified as they went down for the start of the Royal race, when the least expected and worst happened.

The press studs on his borrowed breeches popped open, revealing too much for any demure, faint-hearted females, and the photograph's caption in *The Times* the next day blazed with the irresistible double entendre: *The Outsider Who 'Flashed' Past The Prince.*

"Tommo" Thompson, advertising the fastest Y-fronts on the Flat and more, set a two-mile course record at Plumpton that day, achieving the dream win that had eluded him in 50 other races, plus launching Classified "who was not a nice 'person'", as he rocketed towards another successful career as a steeplechaser.

The Madhatters Private Sweepstakes in aid of charity in March 1980, with 13 runners, including Prince Charles on the favourite Long Wharf, was the last race on the Flat for Tommo and Classified.

Around 5,000 people watched them surge past the post, two lengths ahead of their Royal rival, who was making his debut as a jockey.

Tommo recalls: "Classified gave me the best feeling I have ever had. I will never forget him. He was a star."

The dapper, debonair Derek Thompson, 46, with an inimitable microphone voice, had ridden since he was a boy, hunting with his friend Bob Champion in Cleveland country, where his father, Stan, was point-to-point secretary and commentator, and where his brother, Howard, is now Joint-Master; and also competing in junior show jumping, sometimes in a pairs class with Graham Fletcher.

At 11, he was so captivated by racing that he would catch the bus to Yorkshire race tracks and watch the action from the Silver Ring; at 15 he was commentating at point-to-points; and at 17, riding in them and under Rules.

He became the youngest ever to "call" the horses at the Grand National, the beginning of a busy London-based career, which caused him to quit the saddle in his early 20s. Until, that is, he heard of the Madhatters and 'phoned a dozen trainers asking for a ride.

The only person to respond favourably was syndicate manager Adrian Clegg, who offered his undistinguished new purchase — Classified — considered well down the pecking order at Nicky Henderson's Lambourn yard.

Tommo viewed the bay through rose-tinted spectacles and pronounced him "great". In fact, Classified was merely workmanlike, sparely made, and seldom impressed anyone in a paddock inspection as his coat always looked dull, and he sweated profusely. On the track he was to prove

genuine and consistent, but in his stable he was untrustworthy, ill-tempered and spiteful.

This four-year-old gelding by So Blessed had a month's work with Tommo, culminating in a final seven furlong gallop two days before the race, when the pair roared away by 25 lengths from Nicky Henderson and Steve Smith Eccles, both on winners.

Suddenly, this intended jolly, on a 1,400 guinea Flat racing no-hoper, took on a promising new dimension. The stable enthusiastically backed the horse at 20-1, and Tommo planned his tactics.

"Everything," he says, "went according to plan. Classified led into the home straight first time round, then lay second, closed on the leader round the final bend, and went past as if the other horse was standing still. We stayed on well and I didn't dare look back, as I could tell the Prince was a couple of lengths behind by the crowd's cheers.

"The feeling when Classified quickened on the home bend was indescribable and his power was unbelievable."

Tommo, now notorious for pinching the race from the heir to the throne, was to go on to consolidate his media career, becoming a polished favourite with Channel 4 viewers, who also included Shergar's kidnappers. They requested that he, along with his colleague Lord Oaksey, mediate for the horse's release in secret, dangerous and unsuccessful negotiations in Ireland.

Meanwhile, Classified, testimony to "handsome is as handsome does", went on to win three hurdle races and 10 steeplechases, coming third in West Tip's triumphant 1986 Grand National, where the fences held no fear for him.

Tommo, talking from his apartment overlooking Newmarket's Warren Hill gallops, backed Classified every time he ran, and made a point of saying "hello" to the horse when their paths crossed around Britain's racecourses. He lost touch with the bay when the horse went point-to-pointing in the West Country.

"I can't imagine him being put out to retirement when his time came, as he was a horse who needed to be ridden. He could never have been a pet.

"I went to see him the day after our race to give him a kiss and a pat, and if I had not been quicker, he would have snapped my fingers off at the bone.

"He was a bit vicious," says Tommo, "but a real professional."

10 October 1996

Puff the magical gelding who has a lust for life

Horseman and equestrian sponsor Jeffrey Osborne recalls how
Oscar Papa, his strong, gentle and trustworthy partner,
inspired a life-long obsession with showing

PUFF the mighty gelding was a contrary sort of character. When he was in, he wanted out. Naturally, when he was out, he would not come in, mischievously evading capture by fence hopping around the 90-acre farm.

At which point, Jeffrey Osborne relinquished the chase and cunningly started up the horse box engine, a ruse which never failed to make Puff jump his way back towards the yard, terrified he might miss the opportunity of a lift to a day's hunting or showing.

But when it was time for Puff to retire at grass, he begged to be back in his stable, even when the lorry lay silent.

"It was unbearable hearing him call," says Jeff, "and heart-breaking watching a horse, who had been so magical in his heyday, going to pieces."

Unable to stand the horse's plight, Jeff led Puff in for the last time, brushed off the dark bay's mothballs, and drove him to Gloucestershire, where he loaned him to his chum, Robert Oliver, a Joint-Master of the Ledbury.

Now, at an uncertain age which could be 23, Puff is on part two of his life story, sometimes carrying the whipper-in, guests or Robert, who, on being faced with a five-bar iron gate for the first time with Puff, thought: "Jeff said this horse can jump anything. I hope he is right."

Jeff Osborne, 60, and one of the horse world's benefactors who sponsored five classes at Wembley and will be sponsoring Olympia's Shetland Pony Grand National, has owned many horses — there are 30 in his yard today — but none have achieved, comparatively, so little, or have been admired by him so much, as Oscar Papa, known as Puff.

The 17.1hh Dutch heavyweight, who rides like a lightweight, was the fourth or fifth horse Jeff owned after starting riding aged $39\frac{3}{4}$. He quit flying light planes and racing motorcycles in favour of his new hobby, which took him from show jumping and hunting, where he became Field Master of the Chiddingfold, Leconfield and Cowdray, into showing and scurry driving.

Puff, with a £5,000 price tag, was found at Fred Welch's yard and Jeff, whose company manufactures refrigerators with glass doors, swears that the horse gave him a meaningful big, round-eyed look and the unspoken message: "You are taking me home."

They went show jumping, achieving a clear in the final of the Freshman's in the Hickstead main arena, before switching to working hunter classes, in which their finest moment was a flawless round at the Royal International in 1986, which, surprisingly, the judges did not even consider merited a rosette.

The lowest the pair came in a four-year county show campaign was fourth, mostly picking up second place prizes, with a couple of shows marred by Puff's enthusiasm, which saw him soaring over a wattle fence in one place, and a bullfinch at another, with both fences standing only for decorative purposes.

It did not matter, for Puff was the catalyst for Jeff's showing obsession and, as he says: "They were the best days spent with any horse. Together, Puff and I thought we could walk on water.

"If I was nervous, he took over. If I was happy, he was happier. If I was brave, he was more brave. Talking to him was like talking to another human."

Jeff fondly recalls how applause provoked Puff into trotting more extravagantly, how gentle and steady he was with children from Riding for the Disabled, and how strong he is hunting, always searching for the next fence.

"He is a rare horse without vices," says his owner. "He considers life for living."

Jeff's wife Sally praises Puff, too.

"Anyone can trust Puff in a tight corner or in front of the biggest fence, because you can see him thinking, 'Come on, we will easily manage this together'," she says.

The Osbornes have decided that they will never try putting Puff out to retirement again. If and when the time comes, Puff will go to kennels so that he can "carry on hunting" in the next life.

"Puff needs to be busy," says Jeff.

24 October 1996

The cranky she-devil who hunted like an angel

Quorn huntsman Michael Farrin recalls his seven glorious
seasons with the brilliant and insane Fly By, whose ability,
verve and charisma won his heart

F LY BY was mad, bad and dangerous to know,
toing and froing between brilliance and
insanity.

On roads and fields she bucked, reared and ran
backwards so fast she would almost sit and fall
over; once she nearly pulled her foot off with
barbed wire, but it did not cure her of the nasty
reversing habit. All grooms feared her and always
led her on exercise.

Then David Barker, a former international show
jumper, who was hunting hounds for the
Whaddon Chase Hunt, said he would use her as
second horse one afternoon, quite spoiling his
morning with the dread of piloting her.

No sooner had he mounted Fly By than a fox
was found and David Barker discovered that the
16.1hh she-devil, clad in a brown coat, suddenly
became angelic out in front alone, with hounds
screaming and flying before her.

But he had no need for the mare as his job was
about to disappear when the Whaddon wedded
the Bicester and, knowing of only one other
capable of handling and appreciating such a
cranky creature, set about matchmaking the mare
with a new rider.

At David's suggestion, Fly By's owner and
breeder, Mrs Seal, sold her to Joss Hanbury, one of
the Masters of the Quorn, not for Joss to ride, but
for Michael Farrin, the Quorn's huntsman, who is

due to retire at the end of the 1997–98 season, after
30 years as huntsman. He is an exquisite, gifted
rider, who never seems to move in the saddle.

"Just keep her on the go," advised David, now
the Meynell's huntsman, "and pray you find a fox
pretty quickly."

Michael Farrin remembers thinking: "What the
hell have I let myself in for?" and tried the six-
year-old mare on 8 March 1985 as second horse at
Barsby Back Lane. That night he wrote in his
diary: "The mare I tried today went like a dream."

Michael was introduced to hunting as a boy,
following the Atherstone in the car with his father.
He learned his riding skills with the Pony Club,
went hunting and, at 16, the eldest son of a farming
family of five, joined the Atherstone kennels.

At 20, he whipped-in for the Quorn and, five
years later, became huntsman. Not only was he
one of the youngest in Britain, but considered to
have one of the most prestigious appointments in
Hunt service.

Fly By entered England's premier fox Hunt with
its fast, rolling Leicestershire acres with enough
space for large mounted fields to take their own
line over fly fences and timber.

The mare, by the Thoroughbred Don't Look,
oozed ability, ambition, courage and impatience
and Michael Farrin rated her second best to an ex-
Badminton horse called General Gordon, who

was a well-schooled machine.

However, Fly By won his heart because of her verve, charisma and her "if factor", as in "if hounds check, keep hold of her in case she does something stupid".

While hounds were running, though, he would ask the impossible and she would achieve it, always on the bit and with another gear to go.

There is a wooden gate up a hill behind Harborough Farm which hangs very high, with much air flowing under the bottom of it.

"It was asking to be jumped," says Michael and squeezed the mare, who took it effortlessly. He has not jumped it on anything else since and has never seen another rider tackle it.

The Quorn had a purple patch from 1987–89 and the huntsman, who is given six horses at the start of the season, says: "I could not wait to ride the mare."

One afternoon, for example, they found at the Prince of Wales covert and went away by Baggrave Hall. By the time hounds marked their fox at Tilton Hills 20 minutes later, Fly By had flown over three post-and-rail fences, one boundary fence, three hedges with ditches, a set of timber and over the side of a cattle grid. It was nearly four miles as hounds ran.

"She ate up the ground and sailed over whatever came in front of her. She was my sort of horse, fast and full of quality. She was phenomenal — whether you galloped into a fence, or turned her in off three strides," exclaims Michael. "She always wanted to get on with it and was only difficult on bad scenting days, when there was insufficient action for her."

Michael Farrin hunted Fly By for seven glorious seasons and was the only person to ride her for fast work to keep her fit.

When the time came to put her down, the deed was done by the Cottesmore huntsman, not his equivalent at the Quorn.

"I would not have had the heart to do it," explains Michael.

31 October 1996

The Monkey who climbed the ladder to success

Lady Joicey recalls her top dressage horse, Powdermonkey,
who was "stupid and frustrating", but good enough for a place
in the world championship team

POWDERMONKEY, who was called after the innumerable small boys who carried gunpowder to ships' gunners, could never live up to his name. He detested loud noises and was even frightened of umbrellas.

In fact, this gelding, who was bred for hunting, excelled at dressage, and at five was nearly sold because he was so big, and was not intelligent enough for that simple task on board a "man of war".

He probably would have blown himself up because Lady Elisabeth Joicey, his doting breeder, says: "He was the stupidest and most frustrating horse I have ever ridden in my life. He had a tiny brain.

"You could not get cross with him because he would panic. You had to explain everything to him again and again, very quietly."

The dressage maestro Arthur Kottas handed Monkey's reins back to Lady Joicey during one training session, because, although he admired the bay with a white star, he preferred to exude praise from a less exacerbating position than in the saddle.

Jook and Robert Hall, two other excellent riders, were also Powdermonkey fans from a sensible distance and urged Lady Joicey not to quit. They told her: "You will get there in the end".

The end seemed an interminably long way off,

particularly when it took Lady Joicey two years to teach Monkey to do a flying change correctly.

"I was so near to giving up, so often," she explains.

Her expertise and patience would be rewarded and take them, in more ways than one, head and shoulders above other competitors in the international arena.

They not only became members of the world championship dressage team in 1986, but were the tallest in their class — Lady Joicey is 5ft 10ins and the impressive, big moving Monkey was 17.2$\frac{1}{2}$hh, with legs like four small oaks.

Lady Joicey, a 68-year-old grandmother of seven, who rides every day, is the widow of the fourth Baron Joicey of Chester-le-Street, who shared his wife's passion for horses and hunting.

She came to dressage, like so many in the early days, as a means only to ride in horse trials, but quickly became enthralled.

In the past 25 years, she has taken eight horses to Grand Prix standard, and is immersed in all aspects of her sport, including competition rider, judge, trainer, former *chef d'équipe*, organiser of the Premier League show at her Berwick-upon-Tweed home next May and as a sponsor of the Joicey Dressage Trainers' Scheme.

"Monkey", by the Cleveland Bay Forest Superman, and third generation home-bred on the dam's side, was born in 1971 and, says Lady Joicey: "We were horrified by him. He was enormous with deformed front legs bent over his huge knees. I thought, 'Heavens, this is a poor, astonishing looking creature'."

He straightened out in three months, was never lame and was broken in by Lady Joicey when he was four. Unable to sell him as a hunter at five, because he developed a temporary cough at the time of vetting, Lady Joicey — who thought the gelding moved well — battled on with him.

She had to overcome his fear of new venues and at the White City in 1983, when Monkey was 12, he became the equivalent of today's Advanced Medium champion.

During the next three years, they were placed at Grand Prix level in Rotterdam, Brussels, Fountainbleau, Zuidlaren and Amsterdam, culminating in their world championship team role in Toronto, where Britain came sixth.

Lady Joicey and Powdermonkey were short-listed for the team in the Europeans at Goodwood the following year, after which the gelding was retired.

He was put down on a raw November morning last year. Curiously, his old pal Aconto, who inherited Monkey's mantle as Lady Joicey's Grand Prix horse, became ill a few hours later. He, too, had to be destroyed.

There are reminders of Lady Joicey's former horses at her Etal Manor home, some on canvas, others in photographs.

"I always had a soft spot for Powdermonkey," she says. "We just hit it off and understood each other."

7 November 1996

The Grand National winner who was happier in the slow lane

National Hunt jockey Richard Dunwoody recalls how his
ferocious growl proved the key to his successful partnership
with leading chaser West Tip

RICHARD DUNWOODY MBE was displaying real horsepower at the Motor Show two years ago, when he rode West Tip around the car stands for a photo-call.

"Having his picture taken reminded the horse of his racing days," says Richard "so he began to jig-jog."

The 16.2hh bay gelding was mentally over-revving by the time TV's Desmond Lynam came to interview his rider. The two men had barely exchanged a word when West Tip jig-jogged on to Lynam's foot and broke one of his toes.

"Desmond has never let me forget it," says Richard.

But the jump jockey has forgotten few incidents surrounding West Tip, a Thoroughbred with a pronounced round action, who was happiest in the slow lane, disliked overtaking, and who once had an altercation with a lorry, which nearly ended his career.

Richard, a thoughtful, courteous and methodical fellow, who logs each of his race-rides with appropriate comments, is in fact more readily associated with Desert Orchid, whom he rode to victory seven times.

"The greatest steeplechaser ever," is his pronouncement on the inimitable grey, "but without West Tip, I would not have had the ride on Desert Orchid."

Richard, now 32 and a son and grandson of trainers, was 20 when he had his first race on "Tippy" in the Midlands Grand National in which they came sixth.

Their first triumph, however, was in January 1985 at Sandown in the coveted Anthony Mildmay/Peter Cazalet Memorial Trophy. The jockey recalls feeling profoundly grateful to Tippy for the high profile win.

"He was a real chaser, a natural jumper with intelligence and, like a lot of good jumpers, tended to see his own strides to a fence."

However, Tippy, by Gala Performance and born in 1977, was unhelpful in every other way. He was lazy, idled horribly as a front-runner and was exhausting to his rider, who needed hands, iron-clad heels, stick, precision timing and the Dunwoody growl.

Attempt a long, drawn-out growl yourself, then imagine it delivered 10 times more ferociously and you will come close to Richard's fearsome

Racing certainty: Richard Dunwoody and West Tip clear the final fence of the 1986 Seagram Grand National to overtake Chris Grant riding Young Driver and go on to score their first win of this historic race.

the cheering crowds and quite obviously heartily disliking being out in front alone.

Every muscle felt as though it was strained to breaking point as the jockey fought to keep Tippy running and his mind on the job. As they crossed the Grand National line first, Richard remembers exclaiming: "'Christ, I have done it.' I was in the clouds."

In 1987 and 1988, Tippy made his jockey work equally hard for fourth placings, but he bettered those results in 1989, coming second seven lengths behind Little Polveir.

West Tip, who won 10 chases, later retired to go hunting in Warwickshire.

Richard Dunwoody, the young and inexperienced jockey he partnered back in 1983, went on to seize the jump jockeys' crown three times.

He says: "The year I won the Grand National, I took over the job in David Nicholson's yard, thanks to West Tip."

The equine hero is cossetted and contented in retirement on a farm in Warwickshire, where his owner, businessman Peter Luff, reports: "He has plenty of companions, and goes out with a donkey, the cows, or younger horses."

Adds Richard: "He is a tremendous, courageous character who gave me the most exciting day of my life when he won the Grand National. He can also be friendly and gentle, as with a disabled girl who visited him. She took hold of his ears and nose and accidentally gave him a bit of a torturing, but he did not budge. He will be pampered until the day he dies."

14 November 1996

growl which always accelerated Tippy to triumph.

"Well, you have to use all the aids," laughs the Irish-born jockey.

The pair won again at Cheltenham and started favourites in the cavalcade for the 1985 Grand National, only to fall at Becher's second time round.

It would be Tippy's first and last mistake, because in the next five years, the gallant and friendly bay would jump accurately a total of 142 Grand National fences, coming close to Red Rum as the housewives' favourite.

In 1986, Richard and Tippy tracked Chris Grant on Young Driver and, as they crossed the Melling Road, Richard had a surge of adrenalin and kicked for home. Tippy, however, pricked his ears and started looking about, distracted by

The mighty hunter who challenged the bravest riders

Editor-in-chief Michael Clayton recalls his six glorious seasons with the heroic Foxford, whose bottomless stamina gave him some of his best days' hunting

IT was delivered as a warning, but Michael Clayton saw it as a challenge. "This is not," he was sternly informed about the Irish gelding, "an old man's ride."

Michael, a BBC journalist who had covered wars in Vietnam, Cambodia and the Middle East and calmly completed much of one of his 28 equestrian-related books while pinned down for weeks by Arab gunfire, saw that as a challenge he could not reject.

He wondered later if the gelding called Foxford would turn him prematurely grey?

"You needed strong nerves or no nerves to ride him," he says, "because once he decided to go, he went. He would come up from grass ready to jump the Grand National and was heroic in the hunting field. You just took on everything with him because he was so bold and took an iron hold."

Foxford, by Sadlers Wells, was a raking, strong, prominently hipped, handsome equine extrovert. The late Dorian Williams recommended Michael to buy the horse from Owen Harwood in the Whaddon Chase country, where Foxford was a great performer.

On non-hunting days he was a shocking hack, shying and spooking for fun. He once jumped on to a car bonnet and escaped without a scratch. However, the 16.3hh brown horse never turned his head out hunting. Foxford was superb over the big hedges and drops in Dorset, and voraciously ate up Leicestershire's fly fences, galloping over the old turf with bottomless stamina.

He would jump around 39 challenging fences, including five-bar iron gates and then suddenly miss out the 40th, because he treated innocuous obstacles with a cavalier attitude.

"We had at least two interesting falls a season," remarks his pilot wryly.

One fall happened when Foxford hit a pole in a hedge with the Mid-Surrey Draghounds in 1973, a week before Michael was interviewed for his appointment as Editor of *Horse & Hound*.

They had completed two drag lines when Douglas Bunn, Master of Hickstead, persuaded Michael he had time to do the third. Foxford somersaulted and decanted his rider, who was left wearing the neatly severed rim of his bowler, like a black necklace over his collar, while Mr Bunn was still enthusing about his friend's appointment.

"Just think! You will be paid to do this!"

The Foxford/Michael Clayton partnership took on a new importance, as the Editor adopted the horse's name as his *nom-de-plume* to write *Horse & Hound's* hunting diary.

Foxford was now a correspondent's conveyance,

visiting more than 20 hunting countries in the same spirit as his rider, crossing unfamiliar terrain with the gusto of an intrepid explorer.

Michael recalled an exceptional Christmas Eve hunt in 1973 when the Portman hounds met deep below the slopes of Bulbarrow Hill, a stiffly fenced piece of grass vale country.

"There was one fence which only two or three jumped and old Foxford made nothing of it. I was right in the pound seats for the five-mile point down into the South Dorset Country, with Foxford giving a fantastic magic carpet ride."

Michael Clayton, 61, who is married to equestrian enthusiast, Marilyn, lives in Cottesmore country, is chairman of that Hunt, Editor-in-Chief of all IPC's country sports magazines, and a member of the main board. Next year, he joins the British Horse Society council as chairman of welfare and says he has ambitions to help the BHS "enter a period of fruitful development".

Michael has ridden all his life, beginning as a small boy, riding his first £12 New Forest pony without a saddle.

He declares: "Foxford was the most exciting horse I had the inestimable good fortune to own."

Among the high spots were the completion of the 1975 Melton Hunt Club Ride and successful participation later that year with a Masters of Foxhounds' quartet who tackled the Hickstead team chase competition; only the second year of the sport's history.

The lowest point came when the Animal Health Trust phoned the Editor to say there was nothing they could do to alleviate congenital damage to Foxford's motor nerve, which had degenerated and rendered him a "wobbler". The horse was only 12 and had been with Michael for six glorious seasons.

The vet said: "It is best that we put him down now."

The Editor got up from his chair, closed his office door, locked it and wept.

Foxford has a fitting memorial. His name lives on at the head of *Horse & Hound's* hunting diary, a small-sized epitaph in print for a mighty foxhunter.

21 November 1996

The mare with "devastating charm" who was fit for a Prince

The Duke of Edinburgh recalls his generous carriage driving horse, Brown Owl, whose adaptability and talent led to national and international wins

PRINCE PHILIP was introducing two unsuspecting carriage horses from the Royal Mews to the novel demands of competition carriage driving.

"Short of a burst water main in The Mall," he remarks, "they had experienced nothing more daunting in the way of water than an ordinary London street puddle."

Down in the Home Park at Windsor though, they were first ridden across a stream and then harnessed to a vehicle to be driven over the stream again.

This time, one refused to budge and the other went on, swinging the carriage downstream towards the arch of a bridge which was barely tall enough to accommodate a swan.

"I was just able to turn the carriage without breaking the pole," recalls Prince Philip.

These were early lessons, for the Prince would later become a celebrated whip and he and his horses one of the mainstays of the British team.

He was celebrated not for his Royal status, but for his expertise at competition driving and his knowledge of carriage building — a horseman who was also at home in the world of engineering

with its language of hydraulic systems, flanges and axles.

The Duke of Edinburgh would, in due course, help design a state-of-the-art marathon vehicle, win three team bronze medals, a team gold and be victorious in the 1982 International Driving Grand Prix at Royal Windsor.

Into his sport came Brown Owl, named after the wise bird, and she magnificently lived up to her human namesake — a Brownie pack leader who is required to be "organised, committed, cheerful and kind".

Born on 6 June, 1976, the 17.2hh Brown Owl was a leader of bays.

The 75-year-old Prince says: "She was most delightfully gentle and willing. I cannot remember any occasion when she gave me trouble and she was a special favourite of my grooms."

Leaders can be "naggers" he says, and bite their neighbour, lean on one another, pull away from each other, or be more eager.

But Brown Owl, by the Cleveland Bay Osberton David out of an Oldenburg mare called Osprey, wanted only tranquillity in her pack.

Brown Owl is depicted in an oil painting, commissioned from Barry Linklater by Prince Philip. Brown Owl is second from the left and Prince Philip is on the far right

national dressage test and were in the lead for the World Championships in Hungary, with a mere 26 penalties.

"Until, that is," recalls the Prince, "Georgy Bardos, the reigning World Champion, came in as the last competitor and achieved the unheard of score of 20."

In November 1990, Brown Owl, the parade and sporting horse who had won championships at home and abroad, got colic while stabled at the Royal Mews at Windsor Castle and in a desperate bid to save her, was taken

"She had the invaluable ability to adapt her pace to whatever horse was beside her," says Prince Philip. "She never hung back or pulled on. She had one particularly endearing habit. I give my horses or ponies a lump of sugar at the end of every outing. Brown Owl always acknowledged this treat by rubbing her head against my shoulder."

Prince Philip thought this mare, who was bred by the Queen, was so talented and amenable that she could have excelled in any equestrian sport. Instead, she comfortably slotted in with his public duties and private pastime.

One morning, he rode her in the Queen's Birthday Parade with all the razzmatazz of cheering crowds and military bands and then, in the afternoon, drove her in the lead for a meeting of the Historic Coaching Club.

The Prince, who, as a former president of the FEI, became one of the founding fathers of horse driving trials by appointing a committee to lay down the sport's international rules, had only one dismaying experience with the bay mare.

It was before the start of Royal Windsor in 1981 and he was on his way for a last-minute practice when Brown Owl inexplicably tripped and fell on her knees on the road down the north slopes.

The following year was among their best, as Prince Philip and his team of bays won every

to Peter Scott Dunn's practice, where she died of a twisted gut.

Prince Philip says with emotion: "I was very sad indeed."

His Royal Highness now drives a team of the Queen's Fell ponies and finished the 1996 season as reserve champion in the driving trials' points league, after achieving a third place, three second places and a win in the Scottish Open at St Fort.

He says: "I played polo for just on 20 years, I drove a team of horses in competition for 13 years, and I have been driving a team of ponies for more than 20 years. Quite a large number of ponies and horses have been through my hands in that time. Out of all of them, however, Brown Owl sticks in my memory."

Prince Philip has photographs of the kind and generous mare at various events and championships and she figures prominently in an oil painting which hangs near his room at Windsor Castle.

It is of Brown Owl in her heyday and Prince Philip smiles when he remembers what he describes as her "devastating charm".

"I certainly felt a much deeper affection for her than I have for any horse or pony, before or since," he says.

28 November 1996

The Messiah who was an equine saviour

Reigning Olympic eventing champion Blyth Tait recalls the
exasperating but brilliant gelding who helped him to win his
first medals

IF customs officers ask Blyth Tait what he has
to declare when he arrives in New Zealand to
spend Christmas with his family, they had better
make themselves comfortable. Blyth's list is
long.

After a glittering 1996, the Kiwi — like Oscar
Wilde — will have to declare his genius, then a
sackload of presents, the spoils of his Atlanta raid,
his individual Olympic gold medal plus team
bronze, and he might mention, too, the World
Rankings title.

The 35-year-old Gloucestershire-based trials
rider will tuck the medals in a drawer at his parents' North Island farm in Whangarei, party there
until there are no more corks to pop and, as it is
this special time of year, look in on Messiah and
take him for a hack.

Blyth Tait's life changed with the coming of this
equine saviour. He has to thank him for it and
now only feels goodwill towards him, but there
were times when he felt like anointing the horse
with a bullet.

Blyth used to hand Messiah's reins back to his
owner, Carole Byles, and tell her: "Take him away
before I kill him".

For the 16hh $\frac{7}{8}$-bred gelding, whom Carole
reared after complications with the dam, was
the most exasperating horse in a dressage
arena, where he acted like a grenade with a
loose pin.

Blyth broke-in Messiah and did not meet him
again until the horse was seven, when Carole
asked him to take the gelding eventing. "Mills",

as he became known, was complex and tense.

If he was left until last in the yard to be worked
he would throw a major "wobbly".

It took Blyth, whose father Bob bred and trained
racehorses, little time to work out that the volatile
horse was too quick and bold for Grade A show
jumping, better than average across country and,
while having the paces for dressage, sorely lacked
the temperament.

With kid-glove handling they reached advanced
level in New Zealand, popped over to Australia
to represent New Zealand in a three-star event
and then flew to Britain in 1989 to gain experience
for the following year's World Equestrian Games
in Sweden.

The greenhorns picked off second place at
Badminton and Blyth gave a sigh of relief when
they were drawn for the second day's dressage at
the Games in Stockholm.

"Preparing Mills," he says, "was a major deal."

They spent the free day around the arena, working Messiah in 15-minute spells, allowing him to
graze and then giving him a gallop late in the
evening. This resulted in individual and team
gold medals and spurred Blyth into remaining in
England to pursue an eventing career.

Two years later they were at the Barcelona
Olympics, for which the fizzing Messiah's preparation had been rushed due to a 12-month lay-off
with a tendon injury.

Then, during the time in Spain when they
should have been settling for the dressage,
Messiah became lame again with a bruised sole.

The team vet and farrier got them to the arena but Mills's insecure grenade pin finally rattled free.

His appalling behaviour put them in 69th place and a humiliated and demoralised Blyth had to be rallied by his teammates, not only for the cross-country, but to remain in horse trials. They took the direct route, pulled up to seventh and after a clear show jumping round, won the individual bronze and team silver.

Looking back, Blyth believes Messiah should have been retired then, but, instead, he kept him for another maddening year.

"He only wanted to gallop and jump and if I ever did the dressage at a one-day event in view of competitors tackling the cross-country, it was a lost cause because Mills was trying to chase after them."

Messiah went home to a doting Carole, who lives near the Taits, and is now probably among the world's happiest horses, galloping and jumping in the hunting field, reunited with the person he loves best.

He did, however, manage to spoil New Zealand's Horse of the Year Show cavalcade by his explosive antics and when it was suggested that he join the Olympic parade along Whangarei's Cameron Street, which would be thronged with 10,000 people, Carole laughingly declined, telling the organiser: "You must be crazy to even suggest it."

Blyth says: "He was among the world's greatest cross-country horses", and adds "but also the most annoying. He made you want to kiss him because he could be so wonderful, or clout him when he got wound up.

"He will always have a place in my affections because he put me on the map, taught me so much and stamped the way I have ridden other horses."

In fact, Blyth Tait wonders whether there would have been a string of great horses without the coming of the Messiah.

19 December 1996

The peerless racehorse who played to an audience

Point-to-pointer Alison Dare recalls her winning
partnership with Mendip Express, the bay who helped her
rewrite the record books

MENDIP EXPRESS was like a top model who would not get out of bed for a price less than odds-on favourite and if given the bizarre choice between a cigarette and a feed, would have much preferred a good smoke.

Like many catwalk lovelies, this point-to-pointer was a "poor doer", an equine anorexic who turned his nose up at meals and needed his supplements syringed down his throat. He lacked personality in the stable and was unimpressive in his work at home. However, given an audience, a track and cameras, Mendip Express became radiant.

As a five-year-old in 1983, the bay gelding met his perfect match in a girl who was exactly like himself — independent and difficult to get to know. Together they rewrote the record books.

Mendip Express won 38 times, was unbeaten for two seasons, won seven in a row, next nine and then five and was only twice out of the frame in 52 races.

He helped Alison Dare pick off five of her six ladies' championships, grab the record for the most wins by a female point-to-pointer and equal the record in championships for both sexes.

Bookies loathed them, crowds loved them and fellow competitors, who gloomily saw them arrive in the lorry park, knew the game was over before the flag went up. What made them electric, though, was the pair's unpredictable race tactics.

"He was the perfect racehorse," says Alison. "You could make all the running or hold him way off the pace. As he was such a stayer he could sneak round the inner gaining ground and be in contention without much effort. You could put him in any spot and be in the right place, at the right time."

At Woodford, a young horse ran across Mendip at the first fence, bringing him to a standstill. When his path was clear, he clambered over and went on to win.

At Cursneh Hill, the bay was pushed off course by a runner on his outside. Alison quickly hooked him back, turned him round, retraced their steps and still managed to be first past the post.

Yet there was nothing in the 15.3hh gelding's early performances over hurdles to suggest he held promise. His highest place was fourth in a seven-race career and Alison always believed the skinny son of Pony Express had later to be rescued from an abattoir.

In fact, he had been owned by a butcher and was eventually bought by Wiltshire farmer Patsy Willis, who sent him to Richard Baimbridge to go point-to-pointing.

Alison had her first race-ride when she was 20. It was slow. She was tailed off and thrown at the

last but still could not wait to do it all again.

Today the 39-year-old, who lives in a farmhouse at Berkeley, Glos, is yard jockey to Richard Baimbridge and is admired for her phenomenal judgement of pace and knack of coaxing horses to give their best.

It was a knack much used with Mendip because, as he grew more experienced, he tried kidding Alison he was giving his all.

"The deeper I dug though," she says, "the more he kept finding for me."

Two years ago, Alison broke her leg and defying everyone who expected her to retire, came back on course, wishing there were half a dozen Mendips to get her going again.

"Mendip filled me with confidence," she says. "He was genuine, consistent, had the perfect temperament and knew the game inside out. He knew what I was thinking."

There were two golden keys to their success, which Richard Baimbridge explains: "The first was the horse's diet. He was not a worrier. In fact,

he was as dull as ditch water. Sometimes he would not eat or drink. We had to get him going by 'drenching' him [feeding by syringe] and he would pick up again.

"The second was that the horse had ability, but was so laid back the problem was getting him to produce it. Alison had this understanding with him. Together they made music. I'm sure no other jockey could have got up on the day and delivered those same results."

Mendip Express retired from the limelight in 1992 after winning his last four races and is now grazing with pals on Patsy Willis's farm in Malmesbury, Wilts.

One of his most frequent visitors is Alison Dare, who rode him every Sunday through the summer and is the only person Mendip allows to catch him. Their bond on the track has not diminished now the heady days are over.

Alison says simply: "If he were a person, Mendip would be my best mate."

2 January 1997

The spirited stallion who proved a charmer

Dressage rider Angie Rutherford tells of her partnership with
Lebensmann, a courteous and elegant Hanoverian who
always tries hard

THE wit cast his eye over Angie Rutherford's paddock for her dressage horse and asked sarcastically: "What are you keeping in there? A giraffe?"

Angie stands 5ft 7in in her stockinged feet and the fencing is three rails higher than her blonde hair. This enclosure, more appropriate in London Zoo, is the only way she can keep 10-year-old Lebensmann, known as "Leo", with his feet on the ground.

When he arrived four years ago, she turned him out in an ordinary paddock and then watched in horror as the Hanoverian stallion, who cost a five figure or even six figure sum (she will not say exactly how much) took off across four fields like a Badminton contender oozing testosterone in pursuit of her husband Mike's polo mares.

Leo's next grazing facility was bounded by woods on three sides and a lake on the fourth. This time Angie caught him after he had swum the lake and was elegantly wading ashore, making as magnificent an exit from the water as Ursula Andress in a James Bond film.

Angie Rutherford patiently waited two years to buy this 16.3hh chesnut by Lungau after spotting him as a four-year-old at the Herning Show for dressage horses in Denmark.

"He was performing as if he'd been doing it all his life," she says enthusiastically. "He was faultless and full of confidence and when he halted, his rider climbed off behind, slid down his tail, went under his back legs and came out through the front. Leo stood motionless while 12,000 people applauded ecstatically. I loved him there and then."

The stallion came on the market when he was six and Angie felt sorry for him the minute he arrived at her Sussex home.

"He had this incredible rapport with his Danish rider Borj Rasmussen," she said. "When he went, Leo looked so sad, as though he had lost his best friend. He would see me coming in the morning and look behind me, waiting for Borj to show up. My hope was to establish the same kind of relationship with Leo that Borj shared."

Angie, 40, is married to Mike Rutherford, a guitarist with rock bands Genesis and Mike and the Mechanics. They live with their three children in a former monastery dating back to the 1300s with a moat, a vegetable garden where the monks were buried and a tennis court on the site of the chapel.

The newest addition to the property is an American-style riding complex under one vast roof, housing a full-size school, gallery, 20 stables, horse walker and all equestrian amenities.

Her new dressage trainer is Gary Hoult, a 24-year-old Englishman she talent-spotted in Holland and her horse mastery is a far cry from when she was a child and rode at a local stables in Norwich. This former model is now working with the "absolutely adorable" Leo at Intermediaire II level.

The horse is considered to be of Grand Prix potential, but his rider thinks it is tempting fate to crow about her Hanoverian. She prefers taking each stage as it comes and wishes every competition could be like their first when they won the Advanced Medium at Wellington Riding in June 1993.

They had a succession of second places until their next victory in the Intermediaire I at the National Championships in 1995, followed by a stunning laser-lit display with three other top dressage riders at Olympia where her husband composed the music.

Leo spent much of this year fighting a virus from which he has now recovered.

"He is jumping out of his skin," reports Angie happily and far from cosseting the horse, varies his work with hacking and taking him on to Guy Harwood's gallops.

"I want to keep his spirit. I do not want his flame to go out by constant schooling and being stabled. He is a stallion without an attitude problem. I have never had a bad day with him, and if he finds something difficult, he tries even harder. He is full of squeals, but he would never do anything nasty. He is just telling me he is happy."

Angie, who considers Leo to be a treasured member of the family, took him to Holland before Christmas for intensive training with the international dealer and dressage trainer Bert Rutten.

And the rapport she so craved to establish with this courteous horse? It is there to be seen every morning when Leo's eyes search only for her. Angie Rutherford has even slid down his tail, crept under his back legs and popped out through the front.

9 January 1997

The Priceless eventer who bucked his way to stardom

Ginny Elliot recalls her phenomenal career with a brave and intelligent gelding whose incredible accuracy helped her win a clutch of medals

T HE old gelding, who is known as "P" by those who love him, was a bucking jumper who did not like to be told anything. Ask him to canter or tap him behind the saddle to wake him up and he bucked with the thrust of a space shuttle.

Worse, though, was that while any other horse would have got it out of his system, "P" was still bucking silly at the most inopportune moments.

Once he bucked a mere six strides from the bullfinch at Burghley during the European Championships, and delivered another explosion coming into the first fence at the World Championships in Gawler, Australia where he got in a muddle, had to bank it with his back feet, giving himself a jerk and nearly unseating his rider, Ginny Elliot.

He escaped with team gold medals on both occasions, but then this horse was Priceless in his name, although not in nature. Ginny has, in fact, put a precise sum on the bay, who cost £1,000, laughingly declaring: "He is a guinea a minute."

Together the pair soared to the heights of the horse trials world in the 1980s after being brought together in the late 1970s when Priceless was five, and Ginny, who was then Ginny Holgate, later to become Ginny Leng, was 24.

She and her mother Heather had viewed the 16hh rangy gelding with a small eye and decided

he was plain. However, they devised a simple test by which they would buy or reject him. Ginny would jump him over a deep, narrow ditch and if he stopped or even glanced at it, they would pass him by.

The Ben Faerie bay, who had been hunting with the Devon and Somerset Staghounds, flew across with a dynamic spring.

Ginny, a former Junior European champion, who had fought lack of funds, anorexia nervosa, not forgetting a crashing fall in which she broke her arm in 23 places, bringing a real threat of amputation, was about to enter her senior career on a purple stride.

First, she and her trainers tried to eradicate the Priceless buck, succeeding in the dressage phase, although never eliminating it during the cross-country. It was powerful, but Ginny learned to live with it and, in 1981, they carried home a European team gold medal from Lumühlen, West Germany.

During the next four phenomenal years, they won Badminton, Burghley, a World team gold medal, an Olympic team silver, plus the individual bronze in Los Angeles and another team gold at the European Championships.

Victories were never sweeter especially as Ginny had overheard two selection committee members disparagingly discussing Priceless after he first

arrived and would lie down and rest."

She decided that the 1986 World Championships in Gawler would be the last raid for Priceless. He bucked at the first cross-country fence and, remembers Ginny: "I nearly fell off."

"P" recovered his senses while Ginny recovered her balance and went on to take the championship.

"It was a beautiful way for him to retire," says his rider.

Today, Ginny, who is married to Mikey Elliot, a farmer and Joint-Master of the Heythrop, is writing children's books, teaching and has been competing on a couple of youngsters.

She is the holder of 16 medals, the only female event rider to have won an individual Olympic medal and the only rider to have chalked up three individual European gold medals.

Her adored Priceless became a foxhunter and is now on a stud, owned by one of Ginny's friends, where he shows young stock how to buck. He also demonstrates how to evade capture, but only when he sees his former rider.

appeared at Burghley. They said he was common and would be unable to gallop.

"Priceless never had to gallop flat out," says Ginny, "because he had such a rhythm and incredible accuracy. He took the quickest routes and could save 20 seconds by turning on a sixpence.

"He never had a cross-country fault, a show jump down in a championship and his dressage would have been 50 per cent better if I had not been so green.

"He was brave, genuine as the day is long, and incredibly intelligent. He knew when it was a three-day event because he went quiet when he

"He was impossible to catch in the field," recalls Ginny. "You had to go through a lengthy routine of not looking at him, walking round in circles, putting a feed bucket down and watching him have a sniff, only to run away. It would take 40 minutes. Neither my mother nor I could catch him, though he allowed the girls who worked for us to bring him in."

Ginny visited him a couple of months ago and he came trotting towards her from across the field.

"He almost let me pat him," she chuckles, "and then he said, 'That's it. I am off ...'"

16 January 1997

The mischievous chaser who was like a Thelwell character

Jockey Carl Llewellyn recalls his sparkling, but short-lived,
partnership with Tipping Tim, whose accurate jumping
launched him on the road to success

LIKE an expensive firework with a damp fuse, Tipping Tim's career was slow to light, would flare brilliantly, only to fall away quickly with dying embers.

The one who managed to ignite this £15,000 run-of-the-mill, unknown racehorse was a likeable young jockey whose career was in crisis too. For practically the moment conditional jockey's champion, Carl Llewellyn, moved up from apprentice to full jockey, he was dogged by bad luck.

First of all, Carl caught hepatitis, then, on his first ride back, he broke his ankle and was out for seven months. On his second ride back, he dislocated his elbow and was sidelined again for another three months.

It was a dismal two years and the tonic he needed, he says, "was a good horse in big televised races, and to be seen to be doing well".

What he got, however, was Tipping Tim, the King's Ride bay gelding foaled in 1985. His owner, Jenny Mould, wanted to sell him because she considered him useless, but his trainer, Nigel Twiston-Davies, detected a glimmer of potential.

The white-faced Tipping Tim, known as Paddy, had as little talent for hurdling as a short-legged hairy pony, none of the elegance of a Thoroughbred and all the mischievousness and love of a puppy. Carl Llewellyn likened him to a taller version of a Thelwell cartoon character.

A remarkable transformation occurred, though, when the jockey was asked to school Paddy over chasing fences. They suited the gelding better than hurdles and, given soft ground plus a left-handed track, were going to be the making of the horse — and pick up Carl's career into the bargain.

1991 began with a second at Chepstow, followed by wins in three handicap chases at Uttoxeter, Cheltenham and Newbury.

The following year sparkled even more, when they bagged the high-profile Charlie Hall Chase at Wetherby, to be followed by fervent prayers for rain in time for the Mackeson Gold Cup at Cheltenham.

The heavens tantalised and teased until they obligingly opened the night before the race and on the morning of the race too, and the more it rained, the faster Tipping Tim's price tumbled.

Thirty-one-year-old Carl, who was a gymkhana child and a show jumping teenager, vividly remembers every worrying second of that race.

After jumping four or five fences, the field was going at such a pace that the pair was lying uncomfortably last and remained there as they went away from the stands with a circuit still to go. Gradually, as the pace eased, Tipping Tim clawed in the back markers. At the fifth fence

from home, he was lying sixth and at the fourth was a handy third.

Coming down the hill, Tipping Tim came on the bridle and motored. He jumped the last fence four lengths clear and won going away by eight lengths — a stunning victory from a man and horse who had previously looked like life's losers.

They repeated their triumph in the Ritz Club National Hunt Handicap Chase and three weeks later Carl Llewellyn, aged 26, won the Grand National on Party Politics.

The Welshman, who is now first jockey to Nigel Twiston-Davies and four times in the top 10 of Britain's jump jockeys, says about his favourite Irishman: "I felt Paddy had done so much for me."

He admits unabashed: "I absolutely loved the horse to death."

He praises Paddy's safe and accurate jumping, his kindliness and high jinx on the gallops, which he dismissed as merely the horse's sense of humour. They had developed such a strong bond that Carl could leap on Paddy's back and bring him in from the field without even a halter rope.

But while Carl Llewellyn's own future looked promising, his beloved Tipping Tim's career sadly foundered during the next two years, when an allergy and his tendency to break blood vessels took their toll, causing him to fade from the scene.

"It was horrible seeing a horse of whom you are so fond trailing in with the also rans," declares his former jockey.

Paddy's owner put the horse out on loan, always ready to have him home in his retirement to graze alongside 1988 Gold Cup winner Charter Party.

Carl, who lives in Wantage, Oxon, saw Tipping Tim a few weeks ago when the jockey was hunting with the Cotswold on another racehorse. Happily at the front of the field was his former partner.

"Paddy was loving it, jumping everything. He deserves to be content. He is a special horse to whom I am eternally grateful," says Carl.

23 January 1997

The Tiger of a race-horse who proved to be a pussycat

Champion jockey Tony McCoy, currently recovering from a bad fall last month, recalls his winning rides on Southampton, the lion-hearted bay who started him off on his record-breaking career

MAGICAL McCoy, the 22-year-old jump jockey with the fastest ever 100 winners, was keen to make the right impression with his new guv'nor.

The trouble was, the first horse he was given to ride at Toby Balding's yard on his debut day filled him with dismay.

Tony McCoy is a strong, strapping, weight-fighting 5ft 10½in tall, and the bay gelding was a puny-looking 15.2hh squirt. All sorts of disparaging thoughts were running anxiously through the jockey's head: "He's a pony. He's tiny and I am going to look silly on him."

But Tony was worrying unduly as he had already proved himself in Ireland, and even though he was relatively unknown in England, had ridden winners here, too. What he did not know, however, was that the bay was the most popular horse in the yard of 60 and was not nicknamed "Tiger" simply as someone's idea of an ironic joke.

Toby Balding must have read long-legged Tony's mind because he told him reassuringly: "He does not ride as small as he looks."

Tony and Tiger's initial partner's meeting occurred only two years ago and the jockey was in for a pleasant surprise. Indeed, the whole of the intervening period has been a series of surprises.

The jockey, who gave up ponies for point-to-pointers when he was 12, is now a record-breaking champion. His admiring pundits, including Peter Scudamore and John Francome, say this likeable Irishman is stylish for one so tall, has a good racing brain, is strong in a finish, and is nearly always in the right place at the right time.

Tony dismisses the plaudits and instead praises the good horses he had ridden, none more so than Tiger whom, he says, is his greatest advertisement.

"He has gone from winning a £2,000 selling hurdle at Huntingdon to the £20,000 *Daily Telegraph* Novices' Handicap Chase at Ascot," he says.

On the track the jockey is invariably yelling at Tiger to: "Go on you little b****". Off the track he is all honey to the horse and says Tiger is so good natured that he would trust him to take care of the youngest of his four sisters, 12-year-old equine fanatic Kelly.

Tiger is officially known as Southampton by Ballacashtal, one of whose grandsires is Northern Dancer. Although he is called Tiger, he is in fact lion-hearted and behaves like an obliging pussycat in his stable, popular with members of the 100-strong owning syndicate, adored by the lads and spoiled with mints and carrots.

"He is a bus of a horse," says Tony. "You just sit on him and go."

Southampton in the lead over a fence

One slight difficulty, however, is that he idles as a front-runner, waiting for another bus to come along. Sometimes he is visored to keep his eyes on the green road ahead.

Tony and Tiger's first race over Huntingdon's flights in 1994 was "terrible", reports the jockey, as they were beaten by a short-head. They won next time out at Stratford, then went on to Newton Abbot, where Tony received a severe reprimand after they fell at the last when five lengths clear.

"We were in front too soon and Mr Balding was not at all pleased. What he said is unrepeatable and I went home feeling really sick."

They made amends at Windsor, picked off another two hurdle races in 1995, and came out last year with a flourish over fences. Tony, a joiner's son from Co Antrim, was jubilant over the horse's progress.

"He was improving with age and every race, and was so brave when schooled over fences for the first time. He was really quite manly about it."

The little horse won at Sandown in February 1996, but most pleasing was the gelding's success in a Listed race at Ascot last April, when he won by four lengths.

Tony speaks of his favourite horse in almost fatherly fashion.

"Southampton is a fighter. He's a toughie who has to work harder than big horses. His win over fences showed how tough he really is.

"I will always be grateful to him for helping me get started. I was unknown and inexperienced, but we hit it off straight away and went from strength to strength."

There should be more successes to come from the duo, as Southampton, who has had 10 wins, is still only seven and Tony is keen to partner him in future races.

The only disappointment today is that Magical McCoy, who was nervous about creating the right impression on Tiger two years ago, now rarely rides him.

"The guv'nor lets the less experienced riders on him because he is such a brilliant schoolmaster."

It seems the Tiger only snarls on the track

6 February 1997

The show jumping sensation who kicked his way to stardom

Andrew Fielder recalls the exuberant Vibart, whose meteoric
rise to the top reaped rich rewards — and a huge fan club

ANDREW FIELDER reckons that Vibart's kickback was a similar sensation to hitting the high point on a roller-coaster ride and feeling the sudden plummet earthwards.

Vibart kicked violently backwards over every fence, and occasionally fly-bucked on landing, making a nonsense of any strides his rider had seen.

The affable, roguish gelding, who would stand smarmily and smugly to receive rosettes and trophies, was a show jumping sensation of the 1960s, an equine passport to success with a posse of fans and a hefty postbag every day, filled with adulation.

Andrew Fielder, a 50-year-old construction company director, married, with a daughter of 21, can never forget "Bart", not least because his back is weak, thanks to the horse's antics.

For the former rider suffered the equivalent of whiplash in a car accident an average of 60 times a show, and now visits a chiropractor regularly. He is more comfortable standing in his office than sitting at his desk.

He was 14 and had grown out of ponies — at 5ft 11in he was tending to knock down poles with his feet — when he and his father Jack spotted the reluctant Vibart at the Southport Flower Show.

There, in August 1961, the nappy and roaring Grade B gelding, out of a Clydesdale mare by the Thoroughbred Hyros, had to be hooded before he entered the ring.

When the hood was removed, he reared, roared and jumped a few fences, exhibiting the inimitable kickback, reared and roared some more — and was eliminated.

Andrew was aghast and his sister Tracey, who was to become his full-time groom, pronounced the gelding "ugly and disgusting", but their father could only enthuse over the horse's pop.

Andrew tried the 17.2hh bay and the kickback resulted in his face being neatly framed between the horse's ears. Undaunted, haulage contractor Jack Fielder paid £600, had the horse hobdayed and gave him to his schoolboy son, who spent the following months grappling with Bart for obedience and brakes to stop him from bolting consistently.

By April 1962 they were a partnership and on the circuit. In June, Bart was Grade A and in the next meteoric year was a European team gold medallist and Leading Show Jumper of the Year.

The Fielder and Bart bag of riches, reaped during the following six years, amounted to three Leading Show Jumper titles, the National Championship, a mention four times in the Top 10 list of leading horses, 11 Nations Cup appearances, two Presidents' Cups, an Olympic Trial win, the Geneva, Aachen and West German Grands Prix, plus the Hamburg Derby.

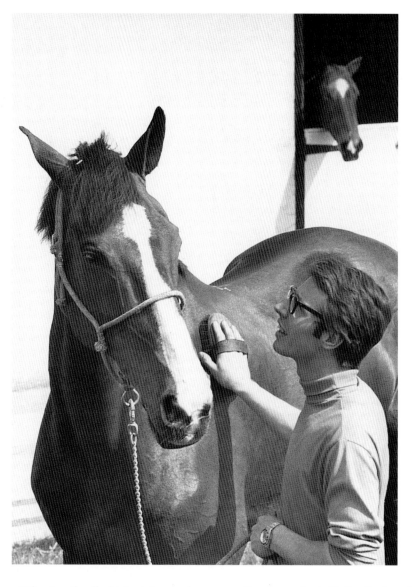

"Phew!" he had exclaimed.

The Olympics were his biggest disappointment. He was ineligible to ride at Tokyo because he was under age. Instead, the team wanted to borrow Vibart. The reply they received from Jack Fielder, a blunt Yorkshireman, was pithy.

"If our lad cannot ride the horse, then no one can."

The invitation was never extended again, so, instead, they contented themselves with crossing the Channel nine times and competing around Britain until the Otley Show in Yorkshire in 1970.

Bart, whose guestimated age was now between 17 and 21, was showing wear and tear on his limbs and when he surprisingly refused in a combination, Andrew knew the horse could no longer make the distances and was tired.

He took Vibart home, removed his shoes and the horse was never ridden again.

"I did not want to see the horse campaigning until he lost all dignity," explains Andrew, who went on to run an equestrian centre before switching to the construction industry.

Vibart enthralled television and arena audiences with his abnormal exuberance.

"And the curious fact was that I became so used to him, it felt weird riding something normal," says Andrew. "He was a powerful, headstrong horse and exceptionally difficult to keep on a stride, but the more problems he created, the bigger the ping. He was not a speed horse, but at the end of a busy year, we could count on one hand the number of fences he had had down."

Aachen was Andrew's most memorable achievement because after viewing the course, he could muster only one word to describe it.

The equine Fielder friend was pampered for another 13 years, until keeping weight on him and worsening arthritis became a losing battle. Andrew, who held him as the vet put him down, declares: "It was like losing one of the family, like chopping your right arm off. You cannot put a value on a horse like that."

Vibart was buried close to his stable, with a simple plaque over his grave. It bears one word — Vibart — and that says it all.

27 February 1997

The brilliant bay who reached the dressage Zenith

International dressage rider David Hunt recalls the glory days
with the eye-catching Maple Zenith, who — between
"gawping around" — swept the "Big Three" championships

WHEN David Hunt bought Maple Zenith, his friends dispassionately decided that the horse would either make or break the man.

But they had not counted on David's nature, which would provoke him into registering only slight disappointment over a disturbing equine matter which would have exasperated many others and had them frantically writing out an advertisement to sell the offending beast.

David Hunt was "slightly disappointed" with Maple Zenith on numerous occasions, since the eye-catching bay gelding was a major irritant, who would eventually produce pearls of performances.

"He had tremendous presence, but his presence came from the fact that he was a wicked little ass," says David laughingly. "You can sum up Zen's life history in a couple of paragraphs. If a flower had come out overnight, Zen would spot it immediately and fix his eyes on it. He would then draw himself up, ears joining at the top and you had to sit tight and hold him or he would leap past."

David calls the behaviour "gawping around" and while he knew the 16.2hh gelding gawped badly at home, and worse out hacking, he never knew when he would choose to gawp in an arena.

Despite the behavioural problem, David Hunt and Maple Zenith, by the Hanoverian Maple Duellist, gelled into one of Britain's most successful dressage partnerships.

Their finest moments came in Rotterdam in 1988 when they won the Grand Prix, Grand Prix Special and the World Cup Kür, making David the only British rider to sweep the big three.

They competed internationally 26 times and between 1986 and 1989 were the first British winners of a Grand Prix Special abroad, won the Dressage to Music at the Royal International, were reserve champions and then supreme at the Horse of the Year Show, were unbeaten in all their Grands Prix in England and came second in the World Cup Kür at Mondorf-les-Bains.

But how did David, international rider, trainer, chairman of the Dressage Group and president of the British National Trainers' Group, achieve these results with a horse whom he cheerfully admits was neither sane nor easy?

"I sweated blood," he says simply.

He was helped, too, by the fact that Zen fixated on fewer distractions in an unfamiliar environment and that David, who was riding for himself, felt no pressure. His attitude was "win or lose, that's life".

Even when Zen contracted a lung infection, marring their preparation for an Olympic trial, David was relieved they were never given a passport to the Games.

"He was not a team horse," he says in understatement.

He bought Zen as a six-year-old, beguiled by his character and zest, and disregarding his bucking and disobedience.

The spooky gelding came out as a seven-year-old at Medium level, and his rider soon found he was in a technical nightmare — and ahead of his time.

He explains: "If I worked him really deep in a 'more round' and 'over the back' way of going, he was obedient and easier to ride, but various judges were critical of this, as they were not used to seeing it in those days.

"Now, everyone does it. What was more acceptable, then, was a higher outline, with the nose in front of the vertical."

Zen preferred this style, too, because, as David says: "He would 'drop behind me' and have me totally stuffed.

"I had to put so much work into him because he was so difficult," exclaims his rider, who was inexorably drawn to dressage while a working pupil in an event yard.

Zen, a talking horse in his stable, even developed his inimitable way of performing piaffe, by throwing his shoulders from side to side, and when David Hunt finally straightened him, the Countess of Inchcape wondered whether he had put him in a deer crush.

"Eventually," says David, "his piaffe and passage were brilliant and he was winning on accuracy and preciseness."

Zen was semi-retired in 1989, and used at judges' conferences, where he occasionally enlivened audiences by following his own agenda.

He had been fully retired for six months when he suddenly developed a mysterious condition which caused every part of him to swell, and brought laminitis with it, too.

"It was terrible," laments David, "devastating to see this wonderful character with whom I had such a bond looking like that. He had a good life and had done brilliantly, and I was not going to let him suffer."

The horse who made the man was swiftly dispatched, and that man wept copiously.

6 March 1997

The stroppy eventer who proved a perfect partner

Chairman of National Riding Week, Jane Holderness-Roddam,
recalls Our Nobby, the joke of a pony who helped her win a
team gold at the Mexico Olympics

THE teenage Jane Bullen found "Loppy's" ludicrous ears handy for hanging things on, such as her brown leather gloves, which made his ears flop further sideways, resembling a moose's antlers.

Years later, she was to adorn one of Loppy's ears with an Olympic team gold medal dangling from its ribbon. Loppy was a plain, skinny bay gelding, with seven Derby winners in his breeding, belligerence in his blood and, at five-years-old, he thought he was king.

He did not reckon on contending with an equestrian family as formidable as the Bullens.

There was Colonel Jack, the father, Anne, the mother, who had an unerring eye for horseflesh, and four talented children. Michael, the eldest, would later ride in two Olympics; Jennie, now Mrs Loriston-Clarke, would compete in four Olympic Games; Sarah, who would play a part in Loppy's success; and young Jane, who was in need of a pony.

The 14.2hh Loppy, officially known as Our Nobby, cost £120 and entered the Bullen ring full of fight. He gave every horse in the yard, plus Jane, ringworm, and brought each of his riders home, including the 6ft 2in Michael, without them completing their journeys.

He and Jane were eliminated from their first five hunter trials, until her mother decided the coffin at the Craven would be Loppy's last stand and, having waited for everyone to go home, had the pony and his partner back on the course, illuminating the fence with her car's headlights.

Four hours later at 10.30pm, after persuasion had failed and an interminable waiting game was in process, Loppy's obstinacy collapsed and he neatly popped the fence.

It was the turning point for pony and rider. Jane, who had thought him pathetic when she first saw him, then grew to dislike him, was about to consider him her friend, while Loppy would never again refuse on a cross-country course.

Two years later in 1964, they won the Junior Members' Cup at the Pony Club Championships and stepped up into horse trials, with Jennie working on Loppy's dressage, and Sarah exercising him while Jane was working as a student nurse in a London hospital.

One day in 1968, Jane came off night duty and, with no sleep, took the crown with Our Nobby at Badminton. Later that year they went to the Mexico Olympics.

She was the first British girl to ride in an Olympic three-day event, and he was considered a bit of a joke of a pony. Together they won team gold.

Today, Jane is Mrs Tim Holderness-Roddam and is in charge of horse trials' non-team training, a dressage and show judge, instructor and competition horse breeder at her stud and competition yard in Chippenham, Wilts.

In three days' time she will see the launch of National Riding Week, of which she is chairman. For nine months she has been striving to fine-tune this drive to encourage more people to enjoy riding. The president of National Riding Week is the Princess Royal, for whom Jane is a lady-in-waiting.

Jane, 49, recalls her lop-eared gelding with one word. "Wonderful," she says and then goes on to explain that he was an independent sort, who did not stand for all that cuddling nonsense, but who was in total accord with his rider.

"We thought dressage was something to be got over and done with before the cross-country fun. Loppy never questioned anything and jumped everything and, as he was so fast, it was a brilliant feeling, hurtling around a course, although it must have been hairy to watch. I steered and prayed."

Our Nobby was retired from competition after the Olympics and became a star, opening the Middlesex Hospital fete, hunting with Jane in Beaufort country and teaching pupils at sister Jennie's Catherston Stud.

The gelding was 27 when he broke his leg in the field and had to be put down. Jane saw him that morning, when he was fit and well, and had travelled on to her brother Michael's home.

When the telephone rang, Jane sensed it was bad news. "I was devastated. He had become one of the family and it was like losing a close relative."

20 March 1997

The model hunter who proved the perfect partner

Merchant banker and Joint-Master Christopher Sporborg
recalls brave and charming Lucky, who lived up to his name

IT is said subtly, that the unwary with pounds in their pockets to spend, do not "buy" horses in Ireland, they are "sold" horses there.

But when it comes to money, horses and Ireland, Christopher Sporborg is a buyer. He is a merchant banker, chairman of Hambro Countrywide, and one of Britain's leading figures on the Turf, a member of the Jockey Club and a finance steward. He holds directorships at the British Horseracing Board, the Tote and the Jockey Club Estates.

One summer nine years ago, he spent nearly a whole harassing week across the Irish Sea, fielding Flurry Knox types trying to sell him horses on three legs.

He was despairing by the time he reached Co Westmeath to view a bay gelding with a skimpy tail which, he was told, had been chewed by cattle.

"I got on him," he says, "feeling rather fat and un-brave and, as I hopped him over a couple of places, sensed this tremendous enthusiasm."

Today, 57-year-old Christopher, who owned strings of hunters and racehorses, including Free Flow (second in the Pardubice), exclaims: "By a mile, it is the best 5,000 punts I have ever spent."

His purchase, Lacken News Flash, called Lacken after the Irish village where he was born, and now known as Lucky, is 16.3hh with a white splash and probably by a Thoroughbred out of an Irish Draught mare.

The 13-year-old's main task is to hunt the Puckeridge hounds on Saturdays with Christopher, who is a Joint-Master. Other duties include being a schoolmaster for any family members and friends who are shaky riders and lead horse for flighty Thoroughbreds.

Nothing extraordinary, but Lucky is top of the Sporborg equine roll-call because he is a go-anywhere, over anything, tough, brave, no-napping, no-nonsense horse, who has all the genuine smoothness and charm that gigolos only pretend to possess.

"Lucky has guts down to his toenails," says his owner.

The banker, who is one of the fancied front runners to be the new chairman of the Tote, recalls a sparkling day with the Blackmore Vale. "The conditions were appalling — water standing feet deep and I only had the one horse.

"We found a fox close to the meet and there was a difficult place to jump to the right, a big Blackmore hedge sitting on a bank, with a ditch in front. Two or three fell there but Lucky flew it, which compared better with my previous visit when I broke my nose after Free Flow stopped at a tiny wall.

"Lucky had a long hunt over grass and hedges and there were only four others flying along. We just ran and ran. It must have been a 12-mile point. He is the bravest, best horse I have ever owned in any shape, make or description."

This former race-rider handed Lucky's reins to his eldest son William for the 1990 Harborough ride with orders to take it slowly and see what happens.

"If Lucky was wrong at a fence," says William, 31, and now paralysed after a point-to-point fall, "he went through it. I came to one fence and he really stood off, then I remembered it was the drop and I was perched round his ears.

"He sprawled on landing and broke his breastplate. I do not know how he managed to stand, but he won by half a length, beating Free Flow."

William and the bay repeated their success the following year and then tried the Melton Hunt Club Ride where they fell while in the lead at the last. They got up, Lucky minus his bridle. William vaulted aboard and somehow steered him to the finishing line across a brook.

It was his 24-year-old brother Simon's turn at Lucky's helm in the Melton last year, where they had to detour away from wire. The mistake over the route, when they were five lengths ahead of the field, put them 100 behind.

Simon, keen to tackle the 1997 Melton, says: "If you were to design the perfect hunter, you would use Lucky as the model. He would do anything for you."

"The thing about Lucky is that he always looks so pleased to see you. I adore him," says Christopher.

Which is why the banker puts his briefcase down when he arrives home after a long day and pops straight out to the yard to give the "Lucky" horse an apple.

27 March 1997

The wild Maverick who tamed the big fences

Show jumper Alison Dawes recalls the strong-willed horse
who took her to Hickstead Derby, Nations Cup and
Olympic glory

ALISON DAWES was so keen to jump in Hickstead's main arena, she would have ridden a goat there, if it had been capable of tackling the Derby Bank.

But what Douglas Bunn, Hickstead's Master, offered her seemed little better — one of his horses called Maverick VII, a roguish rodeo exhibitionist with a reputation for dispatching lesser riders and grooms to a Sussex casualty department, and who had also been ridden and returned without regret by George Hobbs and Harvey Smith.

It needed two people to help 19-year-old Alison into the saddle, one to steady the gelding and the other to leg her up. "Otherwise," she says, "he started bucking and then you were doomed.

"He was a wicked little leprechaun, who thought only of rebelling. You could not school him for more than 10 minutes; a jump in the practice ring upset him, and he was a stopper in combinations.

Maverick's beginnings were no less illustrious than his behaviour.

One legendary dark night, the Irish farmer who bred him led the Irish Draught dam through the fence to a loosely run stud, and slipped her to one of the stallions.

The result was the 16hh bright bay with a disengaged brain and a monumental pop, bought by Douglas Bunn at the same time as his other great horse, Beethoven.

Maverick, aged around eight, was jumping big tracks in 1963, when Alison, a former Wembley junior champion who would later purchase him for £3,000, was offered the ride.

They were ideally suited. She was no technical show jumper, but had an up-and-at-'em attitude, while Maverick needed coaxing, not dominating, and outwitting, not chastising.

They began at White City with modest placings, and no outrageous behaviour from the gelding, whom Alison was now calling "Monty". The napping and rearing in the ring were exhibited later, to be followed by a revolutionary cure.

Alison quietly hacked Monty to a local common, enraged him into repeating the rearing and deliberately manoeuvred him into gorse bushes.

"I kept thinking, 'Do not fall off in the prickles' and he eventually hopped out and never napped or reared again."

In the following decade they competed in 12 different countries, were picked for two Olympics, won two Queen Elizabeth Cups, 103 international competitions, six Puissances, six European Grands Prix, jumped seven double clears in 14 Nations Cups, and Alison realised her dream and won the Hickstead Derby twice.

She declares: "His forte was jumping big fences

in big arenas. There was not a fence built that he could not jump, and the bigger they were, the more I liked them, because it meant we could pick off the other competitors."

Some of those top competitors were generous in their praise for the pair. Piero d'Inzeo informed Alison she was the one to beat, Alwin Schockemöhle called Monty "Lollipop", because he was successfully jumping for loads of money, and Harvey Smith told Alison that Maverick had turned into one of the greatest show jumpers who ever lived.

She was a celebrity, with her picture pinned up in Pony Club girls' bedrooms and accepting glitzy invitations to special events, and a Buckingham Palace private luncheon.

Suddenly the halcyon days were over. Maverick VII, who had been renamed Mr Banbury when Alison turned professional, was retired in 1974 and died violently on 4 January, 1975, when he had a fit and lunged at the stable wall.

He was buried at Alison's family home in Herefordshire, where she planted a copper beech tree over his grave.

"Monty had been there for so long, taken us through those wonderful times. It seemed like the world had come to an end.

"I was not very well prepared and I panicked. Even though I had other good horses, I sold them off and went to live in South Africa."

Alison Dawes is 53 now, and after a myriad different jobs in different countries, a divorce and a new man in her life, she is back in Britain, living in West Hereford

She has returned to riding, with her own small yard and clients to teach.

Perhaps no other horse has had such an impact on the life of a rider as Maverick VII.

"We just had a thing! We adored each other. I remember how he used to nibble my cheek with his lips," she says.

And 22 years after his death, you can see the tears well up in her eyes.

10 April 1997

Index